GUIDELINES

HISTORY INTO PRACTICE

TERRY FIEHN and COLIN SHEPHARD

Acknowledgements

We are grateful to the following for permission to reproduce photographs/illustrations:

- Hulton-Deutsch Collection, page 44 *above;*
- Mansell Collection, pages 14 *above*, 14 *below*, 44 *below*.

ISBN 0582 08825 9
First published 1993
© Longman Group UK Ltd

All rights reserved. No part of this publication may be reproduced, stored in a retrieval system or transmitted in any form or by any means, electronic, mechanical, photocopying, recording or otherwise without the prior written permission of the copyright owner.

Set in 11/12 point Plantin
Typeset by Typewise Photosetting, York
Printed in Great Britain by Longman Publishing Services
The Publisher's policy is to use paper manufactured from sustainable forests.

Contents

1	History into Practice: Introduction	**1**
2	Examining the attainment targets	**3**
3	Progression	**15**
4	Planning: the rules of the game	**20**
5	Planning key stage 3	**23**
6	Planning a study unit	**29**
7	Planning lessons	**36**
8	Assessment	**40**
	Recommended reading	**56**

1 History into Practice: Introduction

In the years leading up to the publication of the National Curriculum, discussion about the teaching of history in schools has always been lively and frequently acrimonious. The main issue of the 'history debate' has been the balance between content and skills in the history curriculum, with one side emphasising what pupils should know, the other the process of historical enquiry and how we use evidence to construct a picture of the past. It was unlikely that any curriculum document which tried to meet the conflicting demands of these two camps would meet with universal acclaim. Indeed the present document has come in for criticism from both sides: from those who feel that the 'knowledge' component is understated – not enough facts and dates – and those who feel that there is 'content overload' with an over-emphasis on British history.

However, it is not the aim of this book to examine the nature and purpose of history in schools[1] or to consider the criticism which has been levelled at the history Order. The fact remains that schools throughout the country have to put the history curriculum into practice. This involves a thorough review of current practice and a complex planning process in which teachers have to build the requirements of attainment targets, programmes of study and cross-curricular themes into their overall programmes of work. The purpose of this book is to help teachers manage this process more easily and more effectively. It is intended as a practical guide for secondary school teachers and those involved in INSET, and focuses on their main concerns:

- What do we have to teach?
- How do we teach it?
- How do we interpret attainment targets and statements of attainment?
- What are the implications of the attainment targets for the way we teach and plan lessons?
- How do we plan a key stage?
- How do we plan a study unit?
- How do we assess pupils' work?

It is not easy to find a clear path through the different strands of the National Curriculum Order and the *Non-statutory Guidance* (NCC, 1991a). Teachers are faced with a new vocabulary and a bewildering number of ways of presenting courses and delivering the attainment targets within the straightjacket of prescribed content. The use of short, sub-divided paragraphs to indicate a range of possibilities does not help. Although designed to give flexibility in course planning, they can make it difficult for teachers to be clear about what they have to do and how they should do it.

This book will help teachers and history departments make sense of the National Curriculum and develop an interpretation which meets the stated requirements and builds on their own expertise and existing practice. Much that is good in the practice of history teaching is enshrined in the Order and close examination reveals that it is not so far away from what many teachers have been doing for years, albeit through different content.

The book's particular target is teachers in a history or humanities department who might want to use it as a way of working through the curriculum as a prelude to planning their own courses. Activites and tasks are given which try to focus discussion around key issues or important aspects of the National Curriculum. These can be used in a variety of contexts, ideally in departmental meetings, and for training days, LEA INSET or in teacher training. Individual teachers may simply wish to consider particular activites when they are relevant to the lessons they are planning or when thinking about how the National Curriculum for history can be implemented in their schools.

This book should be used in conjunction with:

- *History in the National Curriculum* (DES/HMSO, 1991);
- *Non-statutory Guidance* (NCC, 1991).

Note

[1] Many documents in recent years have considered the nature and purpose of history in schools, not least the report itself and earlier consultative documents. A good exposition may be found in *History in the Primary and Secondary Years: An HMI view* (DES, 1985).

2 Examining the attainment targets

The attainment targets (ATs) specify the skills and concepts (or understanding) which pupils are expected to acquire. There are three attainment targets although in practice these may be considered as five since AT1 has three distinct strands.

> AT1 Knowledge and understanding of history
> - 1 Change and continuity
> - 2 Causes and consequences
> - 3 Knowing about and understanding key features of past situations
>
> AT2 Interpretations of history
>
> AT3 The use of historical sources

Each attainment target is divided into ten levels or statements of attainment. The attainment targets represent 'groups of abilities' and the levels represent stages through which pupils progress to develop these abilities. But what does all this really mean and how is it linked to past practice?

Activity

Teachers of GCSE history will be familiar with the GCSE National Criteria and particularly the assessment objectives of examination boards which are based on the criteria.

Compare the National Curriculum attainment targets and the statements of attainment given in Figure 1 with the National Criteria assessment objectives given in Figure 2.

Which skills and concepts appear in both?

Which appear only in one or the other?

Discussion

The concepts of change and continuity (objective 2) appear in strand (a) of AT1 and cause and consequence in strand (b).

Objective 3 (looking at events and issues from the perspective of people in the past) comes within the scope of strand (c) in AT1 although this strand is wider and includes other elements particularly in the lower levels.

AT3 takes in the skills and understanding contained in objective 4.

EXAMINING THE ATTAINMENT TARGETS

Figure 1: *National Curriculum attainment targets and statements of attainment*

	1 Knowledge and understanding of history	2 Interpretations of history	3 The use of historical sources
1	a) place in sequence events in a story about the past b) give reasons for their own actions	understand that stories may be about real people or fictional characters	communicate information acquired from an historical source
2	a) place familiar objects in chronological order b) suggest reasons why people in the past acted as they did c) identify differences between past and present times	show an awareness that different stories about the past can give different versions of what happened	recognise that historical sources can stimulate and help answer questions about the past
3	a) describe changes over a period of time b) give a reason for an historical event or development c) identify differences between times in the past	distinguish between a fact and a point of view	make deductions from historical sources
4	a) recognise that over time some things changed and others stayed the same b) show an awareness that historical events usually have more than one cause and consequence c) describe different features of an historical period	show an understanding that deficiencies in evidence may lead to different interpretations of the past	put together information drawn from different historical sources
5	a) distinguish between different kinds of historical change b) identify different types of cause and consequence c) show how different features in an historical situation relate to each other	recognise that interpretations of the past, including popular accounts, may differ from what is known to have happened	comment on the usefulness of an historical source by reference to its content, as evidence for a particular enquiry
6	a) show an understanding that change and progress are not the same b) recognise that causes and consequences can vary in importance c) describe the different ideas and attitudes of people in an historical situation	demonstrate how historical interpretations depend on the selection of sources	compare the usefulness of different historical sources as evidence for a particular enquiry
7	a) show an awareness that patterns of change can be complex b) show how the different causes of an historical event are connected c) show an awareness that different people's ideas and attitudes are often related to their circumstances	describe the strengths and weaknesses of different interpretations of an historical event or development	make judgements about the reliability and value of historical sources by reference to the circumstances in which they were produced
8	a) explain the relative importance of several linked causes b) show an understanding of the diversity of people's ideas, attitudes and circumstances in complex historical situations	show how attitudes and circumstances can influence an individual's interpretation of historical events or developments	show how a source which is unreliable can nevertheless be useful
9	a) show an understanding of how causes, motives and consequences may be related b) explain why individuals did not necessarily share the ideas and attitudes of the groups and societies to which they belonged	explain why different groups or societies interpret and use history in different ways	show an understanding that a source can be more or less valuable depending on the questions asked of it
10	a) show an understanding of the issues involved in describing, analysing and explaining complex historical situations.	show an understanding of the issues involved in trying to make history as objective as possible	explain the problematic nature of historical evidence, showing an awareness that judgements based on historical sources may well be provisional

Figure 2: *National Criteria assessment objectives*

> 1. To recall, evaluate and select knowledge relevant to the context and to deploy it in a clear and coherent form;
> 2. To make use of and understand the concepts of cause and consequence, continuity and change, similarity and difference;
> 3. To show an ability to look at events and issues from the perspective of people in the past;
> 4. To show the skills necessary to study a wide variety of historical evidence which should include both primary and secondary written sources, statistical and visual material, artefacts, textbooks, and orally transmitted information:
>   - by comprehending and extracting information from it;
>   - by interpreting and evaluating it – distinguishing fact, opinion and judgement; pointing to deficiencies in the material as evidence, such as gaps and inconsistencies; detecting bias;
>   - by comparing various types of historical evidence and reaching conclusions based on this comparison.

There is no attainment target asking pupils to recall, select and deploy information though this may well play some part in assessment in Key Stage 4 (KS4). However, elements do appear in the historical enquiry and communication sections of the history Order – pupils should have opportunities to select and organise historical information and present results orally, visually and in writing, etc. Recall is not specifically mentioned. Pupils have to demonstrate their achievement in the attainment targets through the content outlined in the programmes of study but the role of recall in this is not yet clear.

AT2 is new in the sense that it is now a discreet area with a very specific focus. In the past it has been closely tied in with the use of a range of historical sources in reconstructing the past (objective 4). Much of this – evaluation of evidence, detection of bias, etc. – would now fall within the scope of AT3. So, although closely related, a clear distinction has to be made between AT2 and AT3.

In summary, we can say that there are clear links between the attainment targets and the sort of work being done for GCSE examinations, although the emphases have changed in some areas and there are new elements. Most teachers have long realised the abilities required for GCSE have to be fostered in the lower school. Good practice concerned with the use of evidence and promoting understanding of concepts like cause and change has developed as a result and it is this good practice on which the National Curriculum seeks to build.

Summarising the attainment targets

Since the attainment targets are the very core of the National Curriculum and are the basis for constructing lessons and assessing work, it is important to be clear about what they actually mean. Unfortunately this is not always easy as the history Order is often vague and sometimes confusing.

One area which is especially important is the relationship between knowledge and the attainment targets. The fact that AT1 has 'knowledge' in its title has no significance at all. It certainly does not mean that exercises in this attainment target should be to do with testing recall or that AT1 is in some way more intimately related to the programmes of study. Similarly, the absence of the word 'knowledge' from the titles of the other attainment targets does not mean that knowledge of the programmes of study can be ignored. All of the attainment targets specify abilities which can only be demonstrated through the content in the programmes of study.

It is also important to be clear that, unlike some subjects, levels of attainment are not tied to particular content or a programme of study. So, the same level of attainment can be demonstrated through different types of content. For instance, AT1 level 4b – awareness that historical events can have more than one cause – can be used with work on the causes of the Peasants' Revolt, motives for European exploration in the fifteenth and sixteenth centuries, or the reasons why Adolf Hitler came to power. The point is that pupils use the relevant content to show that they understand that a particular event may have several causes.

AT1 Knowledge and understanding of history

AT1 is concerned with establishing a framework to help us analyse and give meaning to events and situations in the past. It has three strands.

The first strand focuses on the concepts of change and continuity and is concerned with the different kinds (political, technological, etc.) and pace of change. It also requires pupils to understand that patterns of change can be complex and that change is not the same as progress.

The second focuses on cause and consequence and is concerned with different kinds of causes and consequences (social, economic, etc.), how they vary in importance and how relationships between them can be complex, for example how the consequences of the First World War form part of the web of causation which brought about the Second World War. It also includes the motives of individuals as part of a broad explanation of why things happen.

The third strand has two parts:

1 Levels 2 to 5 focus on the features of past societies and how these societies functioned. Pupils are required to compare and connect different features at different times and in different places. It would appear from the fact that this is covered in the lower levels of the attainment target that it is to be done on a concrete level.

2 Levels 6 to 9 focus on the ideas, beliefs and attitudes of people in past societies. Pupils are asked to consider the perspective of people in the past on the events and situations in which they were involved and how their particular ideas and attitudes are related to their circumstances.

Much of this will be familiar ground to history teachers. The use of continuity and change, cause and consequence as organising concepts has long been a tradition in history and has been used very explicitly in GCSE assessment objectives. Similarly much school history has been concerned with describing features of different societies and looking at similarities and differences between societies and in the same society at different times in its history. Teachers have also sought to show that people in the past had ideas and attitudes which are related to their historical circumstances and that different groups in the same society had different perspectives on events and situations. This has often been explored through the medium of role play or empathetic writing.

Although teachers will be familiar with the concepts, they may find the way AT1 is set out in the National Curriculum document a little confusing. It would be convenient to talk about strand (a) as the change and continuity strand, strand (b) as the cause and consequence strand, and strand (c) as the key features strand. However this is only the case up to level 7. After this the change strand peters out and the cause strand becomes strand (a) and the key features strand becomes strand (b). In level 10 only one statement is present which covers all strands. Presumably this brings all the strands together looking at the relationships between causes, consequences, changes, attitudes and ideas in a variety of historical situations. But it is a little vague and its exact relationship to the other strands is not clear.

The different strands of AT1 are set out more clearly in Figure 3. This is particularly useful for looking at the progression from one level to another.

Activity

We interpret what AT1 means through the statements of attainment and their examples. Unfortunately the examples are not always helpful and can be a little misleading. They can also lock us into a way of thinking about a particular statement. This activity is designed to free up our thinking about the statements and help with planning units at a later stage.

Set out the statements of attainment for all three strands without their examples, or use Figure 3.

Collect different examples of current textbooks and/or existing materials in the department including GCSE assignments as well as lower school work.

Go through the tasks in the textbooks/materials and find different examples that would fit the statements of attainment – the greater the range of examples the better. You could also amend existing tasks to fit the statements or write new ones.

Example: 6b) Recognise that causes and consequences can vary in importance.

- Choose three of the items from this list which you think were the most important causes of the Peasants' Revolt. Explain your choice.
  - The Black Death
  - Labour services
  - Statute of Labourers
  - King Richard II
  - John Ball's speeches
  - The Poll Tax

- In a group, make a list of the results of the Crusades. Which of them:
  - had the biggest effect on people at the time?
  - affected people for a long time afterwards?

- Do you think that Adolf Hitler would have come to power in 1933 if there had not been a depression in Germany? Which of the following factors were more, equally or less important in bringing him to power:
  - The weaknesses of the Weimar Republic
  - The Treaty of Versailles
  - Hitler's personal appeal
  - The programme of the Nazi Party

EXAMINING THE ATTAINMENT TARGETS

Figure 3: *The different strands of AT1 (from Diagram 2, Non-statutory Guidance p.B4)*

Attainment target 1: Knowledge and understanding of history

	First strand: Change and continuity	Second strand: Causes and consequences	Third strand: Knowing about and understanding key features of past situations
Level 1	place in sequence events in a story about the past	give reasons for their own actions	
Level 2	place familiar objects in chronological order	suggest reasons why people in the past acted as they did	identify differences between past and present times
Level 3	describe changes over a period of time	give a reason for an historical event or development	identify differences between times in the past
Level 4	recognise that over time some things changed and others stayed the same	show an awareness that historical events usually have more than one cause and consequence	describe different features of an historical period
Level 5	distinguish between different kinds of historical change	identify different types of cause and consequence	show how different features in an historical situation relate to each other
Level 6	show an understanding that change and progress are not the same	recognise that causes and consequences can vary in importance	describe the different ideas and attitudes of people in an historical situation
Level 7	show an awareness that patterns of change can be complex	show how the different causes of an historical event are connected	show an awareness that different people's ideas and attitudes are often related to their circumstances
Level 8		explain the relative importance of several linked causes	show an understanding of the diversity of people's ideas, attitudes and circumstances in complex historical situations
Level 9		show an understanding of how causes, motives and consequences may be related	explain why individuals did not necessarily share the ideas and attitudes of the groups and societies to which they belonged
Level 10	show an understanding of the issues involved in describing, analysing and explaining complex historical situations		

AT2 Interpretations of history

AT2 is concerned with how history comes to be written, how we reconstruct the past, and how different societies or groups interpret the past in different ways. It looks at how factors such as deficiences in evidence, selection of sources, people's values and beliefs and so on, affect the way people interpret the past.

AT2 does cast its net wider than history as a subject and the writings of historians. It looks in a broad sense at the way people create a picture of the past through all sorts of media – film, TV programmes, plays, novels and so on. All these present ways in which the past is interpreted and AT2 asks pupils to be able to critically evaluate them.

While AT2 is the attainment target with which teachers will be least familiar, it is in some ways the most important as it should inform all of our teaching. It represents the view that history is 'the voice of the present as it interprets or distorts or remodels what it thinks was the past'. Pupils should be encouraged to understand that history is not simply a collection of facts, universally agreed, passed on from one generation to the next. They should be made aware that there are many interpretations shaped by the values, attitudes and concerns of the individuals or groups which produce different versions of the past.

AT2 provides a framework in which to expose pupils to the variety of motives which lead people to produce versions or images of the past. These include motives such as:

- to reconstruct the past as it actually was by exhaustive research. Whilst some people would question whether this can ever be achieved, it should be acknowledged that some historians have this motive;

- to create myths, as in the case of individuals writing about themselves in their memoirs, anxious to put their version of the past on record in the hope that people see their actions and intentions in a favourable light;

- to sell the past, as in the heritage industry where museums and sites have to attract visitors. Pupils should be asked to evaluate the way exhibits are displayed, organised and selected, and consider the question of how far some places distort the past to pull in visitors;

- to sell things, where advertisers use images of the past to promote their products;

- to amuse and entertain and to tell stories, as in popular TV series or historical novels. Pupils should consider how accurate these are and how the purposes of the authors have influenced the way the past is presented;

- to justify or explain the present, often used by governments to justify their position or policies.

While acknowledging its value, AT2 has posed problems for teachers in practice. This is largely to do with the way the ten levels are constructed. The main difficulty is that some of the levels appear to have little to do with others (see Chapter 3, p. 15). One way of coping with this is to identify some clear pathways or strands to make AT2 more manageable. It is not suggested that the following pathways are the only ones that may be adopted but they do make sense and they do work in practice.

Pathway 1 – helps pupils to distinguish between fact and opinion, myth and reality. This strand encompasses levels 1, 3 and 5.

Level 1 understand that stories may be about real people or fictional characters.

Level 3 distinguish between a fact and a point of view.

Level 5 recognise that interpretations of the past, including popular accounts, may differ from what is known to have happened.

Pathway 2 – helps pupils to understand the reasons why we have different interpretations of the past. This strand encompasses levels 4, 6, 8 and 9.

Level 4 show an understanding that deficiencies in evidence may lead to different interpretations of the past.

Level 6 demonstrate how historical interpretations depend on the selection of sources.

Level 8 show how attitudes and circumstances can influence an individual's interpretation of historical events or developments.

Level 9 explain why different groups or societies interpret and use history in different ways.

Pathway 3 – helps pupils to evaluate interpretations of the past. This strand encompasses levels 7 and 10.

Level 7 describe the strengths and weaknesses of different interpretations of an historical event or development.

Level 10 show an understanding of the issues involved in trying to make history as objective as possible.

These three strands of AT2 make planning much more straightforward. They also make possible differentiation by outcome, for example in pathway 2, a question about why there are different interpretations of an event may lead some pupils to respond at one level and others to respond at different levels.

AT2 occupies a very discreet area. A clear distinction has to be made between AT2 and AT3 though the history Order acknowledges the close relation between the two. There is no real difficulty when we are considering historians writing about earlier periods whether a modern historian is writing about the Victorians or a Victorian author writing about the Romans – this is clearly AT2 work. Looking at how the American West is portrayed in 'westerns' clearly falls in AT2 and similar films and TV programmes can be evaluated in the light of historical evidence.

It can be problematic, however, when looking at 'how people in the past interpreted their own past'. The history Order is clear that views of the past by people who experienced it as it was happening is a matter for AT3. The 'distinctive focus' of AT2 lies in the way we approach sources of information.

Example 1

In Robert Kennedy's book on the Cuban Missile Crisis, he describes how his brother Jack handled the crisis.

If we use extracts from the book as evidence of what happened during the crisis and to look at the way in which some Americans viewed the events, then we would be in the realm of AT3. We would be considering the book's reliability and value as evidence in the light of the circumstances in which it was produced.

If we use extracts along with materials from other American books as part of an enquiry into how the Americans interpreted the crisis and its outcome (and perhaps comparing these with Soviet interpretations), then we would be in the AT2 area.

Example 2

In the National Gallery there are a number of paintings which have been called 'history' paintings. They show episodes from Britain's imperial past such as the relief of the Siege of Lucknow or an African chief visiting Queen Victoria.

We might look at these paintings to consider their value as historical sources and what they tell us about the events and attitudes of certain Victorians. Some of the paintings are largely made up – contrived by artists who were not present and who were required to add people and certain images to fulfil expectations of what the picture should show. This would be AT3 work.

If we look at these pictures as examples of how some Victorians saw the Empire and interpreted imperial history, then we would, by changing the nature of the questions we ask about the paintings, move into AT2.

Activity

1. Compare the statements of attainment for AT2 level 8 and AT3 level 7. Discuss how these might be different and what sort of questions or tasks would distinguish between them.

2. Consider this statement of attainment: 'distinguish between a fact and a point of view'. Without consulting your summary of attainment targets, say whether it belongs to AT2 or AT3. Discuss why it could be in one rather than the other.

3. Examine the exercise below which is designed to help pupils achieve AT2 level 6: 'demonstrate how historical interpretations depend on the selection of sources'. Which parts of it belong to AT1 strand (c) and AT3 and which to AT2?

    a) Give pupils a selection of primary sources about factory conditions in the early nineteenth century which support the view that factory conditions were bad for the workers. Ask the pupils to draw out the main points made in the sources.

    b) Then give pupils sources which provide a more positive view of the factories (for example, employers' perspective). Ask pupils to consider the difference between the sets of sources and to evaluate them as evidence.

    c) Finally, introduce two conflicting interpretations from secondary sources about factory life and ask pupils to explain how these interpretations may have been arrived at.

AT3 The use of historical sources

AT3 is based on the understanding that we know about the past from what has survived and the work of the historian involves extracting the maximum value from these survivals. To do this, sources have to be put into their historical context, checked for relevance and usefulness and evaluated for reliability. AT3 encourages pupils to become actively involved in this process – 'doing history'. Pupils have to extract information from sources, make inferences from them, assess their reliability and usefulness and be aware that conclusions based on sources are of a provisional nature.

Activity

For this activity you will need copies of the pictorial and written sources given on pages 13 and 14.

The sources on the Boston Massacre give conflicting views of the events on 5 March 1770. They can be used to access a variety of levels of attainment in AT3. But what would be the best way of formulating tasks to do this?

Should the questions be targeted on one level or several levels? Can we devise tasks to show progression through several levels?

Consider the questions below. Discuss which level(s) of attainment they focus on. Then devise your own questions/activities to access different levels of attainment.

1 What is source A saying about the actions of the British soldiers?

2 In what ways does the account given in source B differ from that in source A? Suggest reasons for this.

3 Study sources C and D.

   a) One of these pictures was published in *The Boston Gazette*. Which one do you think it was? Give reasons for your answer.

   b) Where do you think the other picture may have appeared?

4 How reliable do you think source E is as evidence of what happened?

5 Do you think that source E is more useful/reliable than sources A and B?

THE BOSTON MASSACRE, 5 MARCH 1770

Source A

On the evening of Monday the 5th, several Soldiers were seen parading the Streets with their drawn Cutlasses and Bayonets, abusing and wounding Numbers of the Inhabitants.

A few minutes after nine o'clock two youths Edward Archbald and William Merchant passed a narrow alley in which was a soldier guarding the customs house. He was brandishing a broad sword of an uncommon size. A mean looking person armed with a large cudgel was with him. The soldier turned round and struck Archbald on the arm, then pushed at Merchant and pierced thro' his clothes and grazed the skin. Merchant then struck the soldier with a short stick, and the other Person ran to the barrack and brought with him two armed soldiers. They chased Archbald, collar'd him and struck him over the head. The noise brought some young lads together who drove the soldiers back to the barracks. In less than a minute ten or twelve soldiers came out with drawn cutlasses, clubs and bayonets, and set upon the unarmed boys who fled.

One Samuel Attwood came up to see what was the matter and met ten or twelve soldiers rushing down the alley and asked them if they intended to murder people. They answered 'Yes, by God'. Thirty or forty persons mostly lads were by now gathered in King Street. Capt. Preston with a party of men with fixed bayonets came pushing their bayonets, crying, 'Make way!' They took their place by the custom-house driving people off and pricking some; on which, it is said, the people threw snow balls. On this the Captain commanded them to fire, and more snow balls coming he again said 'Damn You. Fire, be the consequence what it will.' The soldiers continued the fire; seven or eight, or some say eleven guns were discharged.

Three men were laid dead on the spot, and two more struggling for life.

The leading article from the local newspaper The Boston Gazette *12 March 1770*

Source B

On Monday night about 8 o'clock two soldiers were attacked and beat. Later about 9 some of the guard came to and informed me the town inhabitants were assembling to attack the troops. I went immediately to the main guard. On my way there I saw the people in great commotion, and heard them use the most cruel and horrid threats against the troops. In a few minutes after I reached the guard, about 100 people passed it, and went towards the custom house where the King's money is lodged. They immediately surrounded the sentry posted there, and with clubs and other weapons threatened to execute their vengeance on him. I immediately sent an officer and 12 men to protect the sentry and the King's money, and very soon followed myself to prevent, if possible, all disorder, fearing lest the officers and soldiers, by the insults and provocations of the rioters, should be thrown off their guard and commit some rash act.

I was now between the soldiers and the mob, parleying with, and endeavouring all in my power to persuade them to retire peaceably, but to no purpose. They advanced to the points of the bayonets, struck some of them and even the muzzles of the guns, and seemed to be endeavouring to close with the soldiers. On which some well behaved persons asked me if I intended to order the men to fire. I answered no, by no means.

While I was thus speaking, one of the soldiers having received a severe blow with a stick, stepped a little on one side and instantly fired. On this a general attack was made on the men by a great number of heavy clubs and snowballs being thrown at them. Some person from behind called out, 'damn your bloods – why don't you fire.' Instantly three or four of the soldiers fired, one after another, and directly after three more in the same confusion and hurry. The mob then ran away, except three unhappy men who instantly died.

On asking my soldiers why they fired without orders, they said they heard the word fire and supposed it came from me.

Evidence about the events of the evening of 5 March given by Captain Thomas Preston during his trial, in October 1770, for murder

Source C

A print showing the events of 5 March 1770

Source D

Another illustration of the events of the evening of 5 March 1770

Source E

> I asked him whether he thought the soldiers would fire. He told me he thought the soldiers would have fired long before. I asked him whether he thought the soldiers were abused a great deal. He said, he thought they were. I asked him whether he thought the soldiers would have been hurt if they had not fired. He said he really thought they would, for he heard many voices cry out, kill them. He said he really thought they did fire to defend themselves; that he did not blame the man whoever he was that shot him.
>
> *Evidence given by Dr Jeffries, a Boston doctor, during the trial of Captain Preston and eight other soldiers. This was a report of the conversation that Dr Jeffries had with Patrick Carr, one of the men who was shot by the soldiers. Carr died of his wounds before the trial began.*

3 Progression

The ten-level model used in the attainment targets implies that there is progression from one level to another. But are the statements of attainment progressive? And what are the implications for course planning and teaching?

Activity

Photocopy and cut up the statements of attainment for AT1 strand (b), cause and consequence. Arrange them in the order you think would best show progression from one to another.

What do we mean by progression?

Is it that:

a) the levels get harder the higher you go?

b) you can't do one level without being able to do the level below?

When you have completed the activity, check your results with the order given in the National Curriculum document. Did you put the levels in the same order? If not, why do you think you put them in a different order? Were there any statements which seemed to stand on their own?

Discussion

Consider levels 2 and 3 with their examples in the history Order.

Level 2: Suggest reasons why people in the past acted as they did.	Explain why the Britons fought against the Romans.
Level 3: Give a reason for an historical event or development.	Select from a list of possible causes one reason why in Victorian times railways became a more important form of transport than canals.

Which is the more difficult?

Quite clearly it is often the case that suggesting reasons for people's actions is a more complex task than giving a reason for an event. It will depend on factors such as the historical context, the materials used and the way the tasks are formulated.

Similarly, is giving a reason for an event (level 3) always easier than showing an awareness that historical events usually have more than one cause (level 4)? Surely a considered and informed explanation of one cause is better than picking from a list of several causes.

So it does not seem to be the case that progression is to do with any intrinsic difficulty in some of the levels although it is clear that some of the higher levels are 'harder' than the lower ones.

Is progression then about having to do one level before moving on to another? This seems more reasonable as in the case of levels 3 and 4 of AT1 strand (b) where pupils identify one reason for an event before they consider more than one cause. But this does not seem to hold true generally: some levels seem to reflect slightly different aspects of attainment rather than some form of linear progression. Consider levels 2–8 of AT1 strand (b):

> Level 2 Suggest reasons why people acted as they did.
>
> Level 3 Give a reason for an historical event or development.
>
> Level 4 Show an awareness that historical events usually have more than one cause and consequence.
>
> Level 5 Identify different types of cause and consequence.
>
> Level 6 Recognise that causes and consequences can vary in importance.
>
> Level 7 Show how different causes of an historical event are connected.
>
> Level 8 Explain the relative importance of several linked causes.

It would seem that rather than progress from level to level it is more likely that you would hop from certain levels to others. Tasks are likely to throw up different levels according to the nature of the enquiry and the questions posed. For instance, you might move from level 2 to 8 in a particular enquiry, or a task might access levels 4, 6 and 7 but miss out 5. Also, you may move more naturally from one AT1 strand to another, for example from strand (b) level 2 to strand (c) level 6.

Activity

Consider the levels for AT2.

Do some levels seem to progress naturally from others?

Would you miss some out?

Do some seem to stand alone and not fit into any clear pattern of progression?

Discussion

Whilst levels 2, 4, 6, 7, 8 and 9 follow on from each other, levels 3 and 5 do not seem to fit the pattern. Level 3 stands completely alone and does not seem to be related to the levels above or below it. Level 5, although related to the others, goes off along a line of its own.

Implications for teaching and learning activities

The issue of progression is very important because it raises important questions about how we teach for the attainment targets and how we assess a pupil's level of achievement in them. What seems clear from the discussion above is that the statements of attainment are somewhat artificial and in themselves do not indicate progression from one level to another although one can see that the upper levels are more demanding than the lower ones. Indeed the *Non-statutory Guidance* (NCC,1991a) acknowledges this when it says (p. B7):

> *the abilities represented by the statements of attainment are placed across the ten levels in the order in which they are likely to be learned. Statements of attainment are intended as a guide to help teachers plan tasks designed to develop these abilities.*

Levels of difficulty

One may introduce the abilities by moving through the levels but one level may not be more difficult in itself than another. This implies that each statement can be tackled at varying levels of difficulty. This will be readily apparent to classroom teachers as the following examples show.

1 AT3 level 1: communicate information acquired from an historical source.

Clearly pupils have to pull out information from a source before they can use the source, make deductions, etc. This can be done at a simple level, for example talk about what you can see in an old photograph. But it can also be very difficult, for example communicating information from a seventeenth century document at A level.

2 AT1 strand (a) level 1: place in sequence events in a story about the past.

In the same class different ways of presenting materials can make it easier or more difficult to achieve within a level. We can take a familiar area such as asking pupils to sequence pictures from the Bayeux Tapestry showing the events leading up to and during the Battle of Hastings. Using only three pictures which have captions would make this a relatively simple exercise. Using six pictures and asking pupils to match these with captions would make it considerably more difficult. Using eight uncaptioned pictures and asking pupils to write the captions would make it more difficult still.

What then determines the level of difficulty of activities? A number of variables can be taken into account.

- Number and length of sources;
- Type of sources – visual, written, maps, diagrams, etc.;
- Complexity of sources – reading level, density of text, syntax, familiarity of language, etc.;
- Nature of the events being studied – are these particularly complex or do they involve concepts which are difficult for some pupils?
- Groundwork leading up to work with sources – how the content is structured;
- Nature of the exercise – how it is structured and whether props are provided;

> - Whether the sources are all provided or whether the pupil has to research these;
> - Organisation of the classroom – whether pupils working in groups or individually;
> - Time allocated to do the tasks.

It is not hard to see why the writers of the history Order found it difficult to specify how pupils progress from one level to another and it is suggested that:

> *It will be the teacher's judgement, made over time and through observing performance in different tasks, whether pupils have demonstrated the abilities identified in a statement of attainment.*
>
> NCC, 1991a, p. B7

This means that progression comes not so much from the levels themselves but from the context – number and complexity of sources, structure of exercises, etc. – in which the statements of attainment are introduced into the classroom. Presumably as time passes some sort of consensus will emerge about what types of exercise constitute an appropriate level for pupils of a particular age through discussion and moderation within departments and between schools. But at the present time it is left to the teacher to decide what is appropriate for his or her pupils and to demonstrate that the activities set allow the pupils to show progression over a key stage.

> **What are the implications for teaching and learning activities?**
> - Pupils do not have to show mastery of a level before they move on to the next level. That is, there is no need to concentrate exercises on a particular level until pupils have shown they can complete the exercises competently. It is not a matter of 'getting pupils to level 2' before considering level 3.
> - It is not necessary or desirable to introduce the statements of attainment in the order in which they are laid down in the history Order. This would be artificial. Particular materials or even topics might make it convenient to bring in higher levels first.
> - There is no reason why pupils should not be introduced to higher level statements early on in KS3. They might meet these in a simple form and achieve those levels, for example two old people giving conflicting oral accounts of life in the 1930s. This might give young pupils insights into the reliability of sources and the circumstances in which they were produced. Indeed pupils might meet all ten levels in a relatively simple form during Year 7 (Y7). The question of whether they can be said to have mastered these levels is a different matter.
> - Levels are not 'left behind' once it is felt that pupils have achieved a reasonable standard in those levels. As part of the natural process of historical enquiry you would rework these levels within different topics but using more complex material and more demanding exercises. For instance, you might consider different kinds of causes in connection with the Peasants' Revolt and come back to this in Y9 in work to do with the Industrial Revolution.

In summary, it is useful to see the statements of attainment as collections of skills and concepts (or 'abilities' as they are called in the history Order) rather than as rigid levels. Unfortunately, the ten-level model seems to suggest a series of steps where the lower steps have to be climbed before you can get to the top. This is misleading and could result in teaching which is artificial and pedestrian. It is better to think of the statements as skills and concepts which teachers will introduce and spiral back to again and again throughout a key stage in different contexts and in different degrees of complexity. The task for the teacher is to devise materials and teaching strategies which will do this in a variety of ways. This will have to be built into units of work and thus places greater emphasis on the planning of the programmes of study.

4 Planning: the rules of the game

The prescriptive nature of the history Order does not mean that teachers have had the burden of planning courses removed from them. There is just as much planning to do as in the past and in many ways it is more complex: teachers have to make explicit the relationship between the various elements of the National Curriculum – content, attainment targets, resources, assessment, cross-curricular links and so on.

Planning ranges from planning a key stage in outline right through to individual lesson plans – and there are many stages inbetween. It is an ongoing process in which schemes of work are refined and adjusted as programmes of study are implemented. The aim of this chapter is to help teachers begin this process and to offer some ideas for ways of selecting and planning units for KS3.

What are the requirements of the National Curriculum for KS3?

The core study units

Eight study units have to be covered in the three-year period.

- Five core units:
  - The Roman Empire
  - Medieval Realms: Britain 1066 to 1500
  - The Making of the United Kingdom: Crowns, Parliaments and People, 1500 to 1750
  - Expansion, Trade and Industry: Britain 1750 to 1900
  - The Era of the Second World War

- Three supplementary units which must:
  - complement or extend the core units;
  - make demands comparable to those of a core study unit in terms of knowledge, understanding and skills.

The supplementary units

One unit must be chosen from each of the following categories.

A. A British study unit which should:

- relate to the history of the British Isles before 1920;
- involve a study in depth or a study of a theme over a long period of time.

B. A study unit involving a episode or turning point in European history. It should:

- be based on an episode or turning point of major historical importance;
- illustrate links between developments in different parts of Europe;
- examine the short- and long-term impact of the episode or turning point.

C. A unit involving the study of a past non-European society. This should:

- focus on key historical issues concerning people of non-European background in a past society in Asia, Africa, America or Australia;
- involve study from a variety of perspectives – political, economic, technological, social, religious, cultural and aesthetic;
- involve study of the society over a long period of time;
- be based on a society different from those in category C in KS2.

Examples of units which could be studied can be found in the National Curriculum Order but teachers do not have to choose units from the list of examples. They can create units which are entirely of their own making as long as they cover the three categories set out above and conform to the criteria in each category.

Rules about the ordering of the core unit

- The core study units, apart from the Roman Empire, must be taught in chronological order.
- There must be at least one of these units in each year.
- The Roman Empire, like the supplementary units, can be taught at any time.

This does not really leave a great deal of choice as the grid below shows.

Year	Core study unit
7	Medieval Realms
8	The Making of the UK
	Expansion, Trade and Industry
9	The Era of the Second World War

Since a core study unit must be taught in each year, three of the core units above have to be taught in successive years. Expansion, Trade and Industry is the only unit which offers flexibility; it can appear in Y8 or Y9. However, if Expansion, Trade and Industry becomes a unit to which Standard Assessment Tests (SATs) are applied, then most teachers will probably want to put it in Y9 in order to teach it as close to the SATs as possible. This also raises the question of how to deploy eight units in the nine terms of KS3. It seems that the choice is likely to be between:

1 Two units in Y7 with perhaps an introductory unit on What is History?   *or*   2 Two units in Y9 when pupils will take the SATs, devoting the time before the SATs to the areas pupils will be tested on.

5 Planning key stage 3

Within the constraints imposed by the Order, teachers have to decide where they are going to put the Roman Empire and how to select the supplementary units from categories A, B and C. Given that it is undesirable that pupils should jump from one area of content to another without any apparent links between units, it follows that some unifying or organising ideas are required for each year. These will provide the criteria for the selection and ordering of units and coherence for the key stage as a whole.

Organising ideas

There are, of course, many different ways in which the units can be organised and different organising or unifying ideas on which the selection can be made. Some models are suggested below. The first examples keep the units discrete but allow for links between them; the later ones break the integrity of the units to suggest other ways of organising them.

Approaches which keep the units discrete

1 Year 7	Organising idea: how people lived
Roman Empire	The focus across the three units would be on the similarities and differences between the different societies in areas such as: • people's lives at home; • how they were governed.
Medieval Realms	• the role of religion; • how 'civilised' they were (different concepts of being civilised); • health and medicine; • art and architecture.
Islamic Societies	There are many other ways of making links and contrasting the societies. For instance, the impact that these societies had on each other could be examined.

2	**Year 8**	**Organising idea: revolutions**
	The Making of the UK	The focus across the three units would be on an examination of different types of revolution. These units contain:
		▪ French Revolution
		▪ English Revolution
		▪ Glorious Revolution
	French Revolution	▪ Industrial Revolution
		▪ Agricultural Revolution
		▪ Scientific Revolution
		Issues which arise could include:
		▪ how are these all revolutions?
		▪ what do they have in common?
	Expansion, Trade and Industry	▪ what causes and ideals are involved?
		▪ the course and nature of the revolution;
		▪ what consequences did they have?
		▪ the role of individuals in them.

3	**Year 9**	**Organising idea: the impact of wars**
	Britain and the Great War 1914–1918	These could focus on:
		▪ the changing nature of warfare;
		▪ attitudes to war, propaganda, how civilians reacted;
	The Era of the Second World War	▪ social consequences – changing role of women;
		▪ political and economic effects;
		▪ war art and culture.
		In particular, pupils could examine how the consequences of the First World War could contribute to causes of the Second World War.

> **4** A year could be built around the theme of empires.
>
> | Year ? | Organising idea: empires |
> |---|---|
> | Choose three units from the following list: | These could focus on issues such as: |
> | Roman Empire
British Empire
Mughal Empire in India
Imperial China
Islamic Empire | ▪ nature of imperial rule and administration;
▪ how established control;
▪ impact on subjected peoples;
▪ influence on culture, religion;
▪ role of women;
▪ reasons for success/decline;
▪ achievements/legacy. |

Other examples of organising themes might be 'conquest' or 'the impact of industrialisation'. It is not suggested that every lesson should be spent hammering away at the theme/focus; rather that it is explored at points during the programme of study. Comparative exercises/studies can be carried out when appropriate, and the strands of the theme can be brought together at the end. Studying a range of examples can help pupils develop their understanding of concepts like 'empire' or 'revolution' and the use of an organising idea does give coherence and shape to the year.

Activity

Take different concepts or organising ideas and plan out a year's course. Play with various combinations of units to devise a course for the three years of KS3.

One way of doing this is to write the names of units on strips of paper and then arrange them in various combinations according to the themes selected. It is also helpful to keep in mind the constraints of the Order – chronological ordering of core units, one in each year, categories A, B and C, etc.

Other approaches

5 It is possible to incorporate a supplementary unit in a core unit. There are some places where this would work well such as:

Castles and Cathedrals ⟶ Medieval Realms
Crusades ⟶ Medieval Realms
Crusades ⟶ Islamic Civilisations
Reformation ⟶ Making of the UK
Impact of Industrial Revolution on local area ⟶ Expansion, Trade and Industry

However, it is important to remember that if the supplementary unit is incorporated within a core unit, it must still be possible to show the details of the unit separately. For example, the programme of study for Castles and Cathedrals should be available even if it is delivered through Medieval Realms. This is a requirement of the Order.

6 A supplementary unit can be collapsed across other units in the key stage. This is a good way of dealing with the pressure of the content loading of the National Curriculum. For example, a supplementary unit (category A), such as the Changing Role of Women Through Time, could be delivered through the other units.

Year 7	**Role of Women**
Medieval Realms	Position of women in medieval Britain – in town and countryside.
Roman Empire	Comparative work on position of women in Roman society.
Year 8	
Making of the UK	A study of queens and their power in the sixteenth century. Changes in family relationships during this period. Role of women in society.
French Revolution	Women as active participants in revolution, ideas of equality.
Indigenous Peoples of North America	Role of women in a non-European society.
Year 9	
Expansion, Trade and Industry	Impact of industrialisation on the role of women emphasising women at work and women's movements.
The Era of the Second World War	Position of women in the 1930s. Participation in war. Effect of war on the role/status of women.

Other themes could be chosen to draw out throughout the key stage – medicine, entertainment, crime and punishment, and so on.

7 A supplementary unit could be split into two parts and taught in successive years, say Y8 and Y9. For example,

Year 8

The Making of the UK

Culture and Society in Ireland, part 1 (early times to 1750)

French Revolution

Year 9

Expansion, Trade and Industry

Era of the Second World War

Culture and Society in Ireland, part 2 (1750–twentieth century)

Other topics in a category A British supplementary unit which could be split in this way might be:

- Poverty in Britain, part 1 sixteenth–seventeenth centuries
  part 2 nineteenth–twentieth centuries

- Colonialism and Empire, part 1 sixteenth–eighteenth centuries,
  part 2 nineteenth–twentieth centuries

8 Cross-curricular themes can be used as organising ideas or as connecting points across units. Even if teachers do not use this as a basis for constructing units it is important to pull these out for comparative purposes and to meet the requirements of the Order in this respect. For instance, if pupils were studying the Roman Empire, Medieval Realms and the Islamic Empire in Y7, then comparative lessons could be set up using the cross-curricular themes/issues below or each could be studied separately in its own unit and comparative points drawn out by the teacher by referring back to other units. The following box contains two examples.

Citizenship

- How were people governed?   Emphasis on how people affected in their daily lives.

- How civilised were they? (Including how citizens and minorities were treated.)   Definition of 'civilised' and learning, art, science, technology, etc. Crime and punishment, slavery, treatment of conquered peoples, etc.

- What were the problems of being in charge?   Roman emperor, caliph and king of England

Economic and Industrial Understanding

- How were they fed and supplied?   How Rome, London and Baghdad were fed – economic organisation to do this.

- How was industry organised?   Level of technology, crafts, etc.

Supplementary units, as well as being important in themselves in introducing European, and non-Western perspectives to the history curriculum, can be used as key organising devices to create a coherent year's course. Supplementary units can be used to provide contrasts, for example Medieval Realms and Islamic Societies. Teachers and pupils could consider the similarities and differences between the two societies – religious beliefs, government, lives of ordinary people, etc. – to deepen understanding of both and link the two units.

Supplementary units can be integrated in core units, for example Crusades in Medieval Realms, or scattered across a whole key stage, for example Women Through Time (see p. 26). Local history can be included as a local aspect of each British core unit; taken together these local aspects would form a British supplementary unit. Supplementary units can be used to bridge core units, for example the gap between Expansion, Trade and Industry and the Era of the Second World War could be bridged by Britain and the Great War.

The point being made here is that supplementary units, rather than being seen as add-ons, can be used creatively to break down the block-like structure of the National Curriculum and provide a more fluent and coherent course for pupils.

Activity

This is an extension of the first activity in this chapter (p. 25) and might be done at the same time.

1 Consider the existing resources in your department – books and your own materials – together with the expertise and areas of interest of departmental members. Decide how these might be used in KS3 units and also how specific school constraints, such as time allocation for Years 7, 8 and 9, will impinge on National Curriculum history. Consider also the cultural background of the local community and what opportunities the local area can offer for certain units such as fieldwork, local historical sites or buildings, museum visits, which would permit varied and stimulating kinds of teaching.

2 Draw up alternative ways of covering the core units and supplementary units using some of the ideas in examples 1–8 above. Bear in mind the interests/expertise/constraints identified in the department and the character of the local community. This may mean devising new supplementary units (the ones suggested in the history Order are only examples and are not mandatory). Devise a first draft of a plan for the whole of KS3.

6 Planning a study unit

There is not really much difference in the planning required for a core study or a supplementary unit. The programme of study for a core unit tells us only what areas have to be covered; it does not represent a course or a scheme of work. It is the raw material from which a course can be fashioned. So a scheme of work has to be drawn up in much the same way for core and supplementary units. The only other distinguishing feature of a core unit is that it has a particular focus which must play a part in the planning.

In supplementary units teachers can determine the focus and the content as long as the unit makes similar demands (content, skills, understanding) as a core unit and conforms to the criteria of the three categories A, B and C.

One of the main problems of planning core units is the amount of content in the programmes of study. If an attempt is made to cover all of the content in the same degree of depth, then one of two things is likely to happen: either the teacher will run out of time and the unit will not be completed or each area of content will be covered so superficially that it will be of little value to pupils. Both scenarios could lead to a race through content 'which has to be covered', making it doubtful that the attainment targets would be accessed in a meaningful way.

This means that there must be selection. It will be necessary to focus in depth on some parts of the programme of study and cover other areas of content more quickly. This is perfectly legitimate and indeed is part of good planning.

When planning units it is important to bear in mind that across the key stage or in any one year, pupils should cover the content from a variety of perspectives – political, economic, technological and scientific, social, religious, cultural and aesthetic – although these do not have to be delivered in every unit. Similarly, pupils should be introduced to a full range of historical sources (identified in the history Order) although the types of sources they meet in any one unit will depend on the nature of the unit and what is available.

Linking units to the attainment targets

Planning a unit must involve a partnership between content and attainment targets. Teaching a unit in blocks of content is likely to lead to sterile history lessons and will not naturally lead on to work which accesses the attainment targets. Nor is it desirable that units should be attainment target-led. This could lead to an over-emphasis on measurement of achievement and to interesting information or issues being missed out. It also might mean that teachers abandon stimulating or enjoyable lessons (for example decison-making exercises) because they don't fit into the structure of the attainment targets.

Using key questions and real historical issues

One way to achieve a balance between content and attainment targets, and at the same time develop a stimulating approach to programmes of study, is to plan a unit around real historical issues. Choosing interesting issues and formulating key questions about these also puts the teacher in control of the programme of study rather than the other way round. What is more, when you check your issues/key questions against the content of the study unit, you will probably find that some items have been covered more than once while others have been covered briefly. This does not matter, but if you feel you want to re-balance the unit or bring in a part of the programme which has been missed out, then this is easy to do. The teacher should provide the links between the key questions to make sense of the unit as a whole. Consider the example given in Figure 4.

The advantage of this approach is that it is easier to link the content with the attainment targets. Each issue or enquiry quite naturally accesses an attainment target. This gives the enquiry a clear focus but it does not mean that only one attainment target will be covered in the enquiry. As the enquiry is fleshed out other attainment targets or strands will come in. In Figure 5, for example, AT3 does not appear frequently but it will certainly feature heavily as the enquiry is turned into lesson plans and teaching materials.

The advantages of using key questions as a device for organising study units can be summarised as follows.

- They provide pathways through the content, preventing units being a line-by-line trot through the content of the programme of study.
- They prevent planning and teaching being assessment-led and help to ensure, by focusing reach key question on one attainment target, that the attainment targets are accessed.
- They encourage an investigative approach which motivates pupils.
- They show that the study of history is problematic, that is a process of posing questions and using evidence to reach provisional answers.

Matrix

When preparing a unit, the various requirements of the National Curriculum have to be taken into account and the different elements shown in relation to each other. The best way of making sure that everything has been covered is to set out the unit on a matrix. There are several examples of matrices in the *Non-statutory Guidance* (NCC, 1991a). It is suggested that the following elements should be included in the grid:

- key themes, questions and hypotheses (enquiries)
- concepts
- content
- resources
- activities
- teaching and learning methods
- attainment targets
- cross-curricular links

However, although it is useful to have this as a checklist, it can be difficult to use this format as a practical planning aid. Figure 5 on Britain and the American Revolution presents a simplified version.

PLANNING A STUDY UNIT

Figure 4: *Linking the content of a topic with the attainment target: the Roman Empire*

THE ROMAN EMPIRE KS3: core study unit 1 **Programme of study statements**	Issues/key questions	How did the Roman Empire begin?	Why was Caesar murdered?	How was Rome fed?	How different was life in Rome from life in the provinces?	Why was Britain invaded and conquered?	How was the Empire controlled?	How civilised were the Romans?	Why did the Western Empire collapse and the Eastern Empire survive?
The formation of the Roman Empire, including the reign of Emperor Augustus		✓	✓						
The expansion of the Roman Empire		✓				✓			
The nature of imperial rule						✓	✓		
The barbarian invasions, the sack of Rome, AD 410, and the survival of the Empire in the East									✓
Rome's dependence on the provinces				✓					
Trade and communications				✓					
Roman technology, including roads and water systems				✓					
Ways of life in Rome and the provinces					✓			✓	
Family and society					✓			✓	
Religion in the Empire, including Emperor Constantine and the development of Christianity								✓	
Roman art and architecture								✓	
Roman literature and the importance of the Latin language								✓	
The influence of Roman Culture on European civilisation								✓	
	AT focus	AT1 (a), (c)	AT1 (b), (c) AT3	AT1 (c)	AT1 (c) AT3	AT1 (b), (c)	AT1 (b), (c)	AT2 AT3	AT1 (b)

Figure 5: *A practical planning aid to the study of the American Revolution*
BRITAIN AND THE AMERICAN REVOLUTION   KS3: supplementary study unit. Focus: how the American people gained their independence.

Key issues	Content	Activities/teaching and learning methods	Resources	Attainment targets
What was the relationship between Britain and America before the revolution?	Origins and establishment of the 13 colonies. Relation to French and Spanish colonies.	Brainstorm reasons for migration today. Compare with motives of early migrants to America – similarities and differences. Mapwork: development of 13 colonies and relation to French and Spanish colonies.	Film, textbooks, sources about migrants. Maps of North America at different times.	AT1(b) AT1(a)
What was life like in the colonies?	Social and economic differences between colonies. Position of black slaves and native Americans.	Research/group work – groups allocated two/three colonies; investigate lifestyle; present findings to class. Comparison. Teacher-led enquiry: advantages and disadvantages to mother country.	Textbooks and library books. Prepared worksheets with variety of written sources.	AT1(c) AT3
How did the British control the colonies?	Colonial government, army, trade and industry.			
What were the causes of the revolution?	Political (representation, British control, political ideals, etc.) Economic (taxes, customs duties, British industrial protection, etc.) Expansion westwards.	Analysis of grievances through range of sources. Pupils write letter to British Parliament setting out political and economic grievances.	Textbooks, political cartoons, American/British views.	AT1(b) AT2 AT3
How did the revolution begin?	Boston Massacre.	Pupils study conflicting accounts of the Boston Massacre: consider bias, propaganda and circumstances in which accounts produced.	Pictorial and written sources.	AT3 AT2
	Boston Tea Party, Declaration of Rights, Coercive Acts, Lexington.	Writing causal account – different kinds of causes (political/economic, long/short term), interrelationship between different factors.	As above, and interpretations by historians.	AT1(b) AT2
	Declaration of Independence.	Discussion on individual rights and liberties and role of the state.	Extracts from Declaration of Independence.	
Did all Americans support the revolution?	Loyalists v. revolutionaries. Role of women. Position of blacks, native Americans.	Role play – in different roles pupils have to decide which side to support, then have to convince waverers by putting argument for their side.	Film 'Revolution', extracts from supporters of both sides.	AT2 AT3 AT1(c)
What happened during the war?	Main events of war.	Investigation of American chances of winning in early stages of war. Use annotated map of campaigns and main battles to draw up timeline of war. Selected accounts of views of conduct of war. Case study of one battle (probably Yorktown).	Textbooks, primary and secondary sources, and maps.	AT1(a) AT3
Why did the British lose the war?	Factors: problems of communication and supply, leadership, changes in Continental Army, other countries, etc.	Prioritising exercise to consider relative importance of factors – whether a British failure or American victory. Structured account.	Textbooks, library books.	AT1(b) AT2
What were the consequences of the revolution?	Impact on: a) America (constitution, state government, expansion westwards, etc.) b) Britain (government, trade, etc.) c) Europe – particularly France.	Investigation of how things were different in America after war. Consider how consequences of one event can cause other changes.	Historical interpretations – contemporary and modern.	AT1(b) AT2 AT3

The advantage of this simplified layout is that it is highly focused on practical delivery – the issue we are examining, the content involved, how we teach it, the resources we need and how this links to the attainment targets. The other elements, such as concepts or cross-curricular links can be drawn out afterwards and added to a matrix. Concepts which could be developed in the American Revolution example could include: migration, settlement, colonialism, parliamentary representation, revolution, individual rights and liberties, leadership, patriotism, constitution and so on. Cross-curricular links are apparent for geography (migration and settlement to North America) and English (role-play on which side to join and opportunities for structured writing, such as causal account). There will also be opportunities to deliver cross-curricular themes such as EIU (economic position of colonies) and citizenship (role of state, rights and duties of individuals).

A different approach

This does not mean that teachers are restricted to the matrix format. There is no reason why more creative ways of planning units should not be employed as long as the programme of study is covered. Figure 6 provides an example of a different approach to devising a study unit. Here the Medieval Realms unit has been planned around the central theme of a single village. This could be a real village, perhaps a local one if records exist, or a composite one built up from source material. The village should contain identifiable people and be given a physical representation.

Figure 6: *A different approach to devising a study unit*

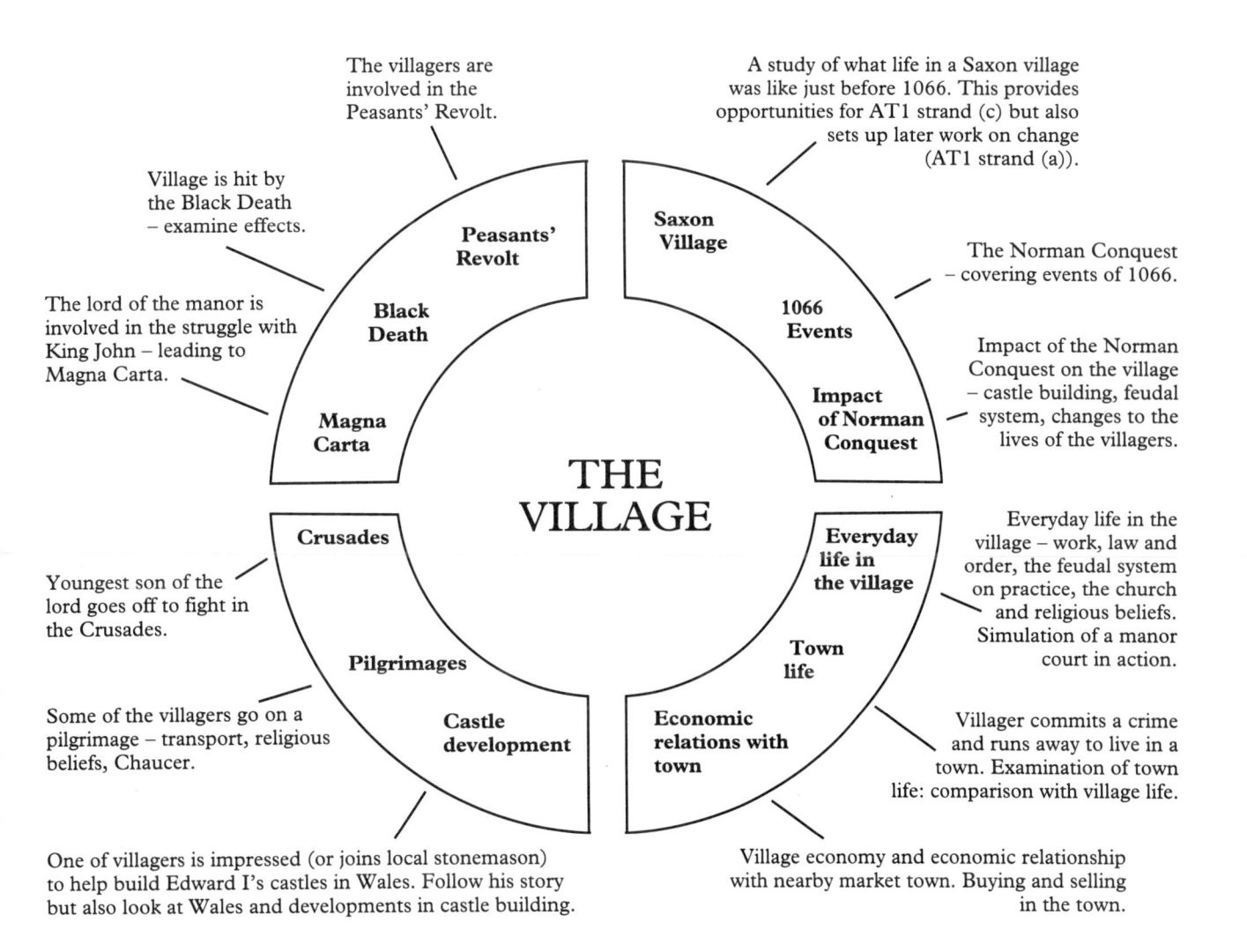

- The villagers are involved in the Peasants' Revolt.
- A study of what life in a Saxon village was like just before 1066. This provides opportunities for AT1 strand (c) but also sets up later work on change (AT1 strand (a)).
- Village is hit by the Black Death – examine effects.
- The Norman Conquest – covering events of 1066.
- The lord of the manor is involved in the struggle with King John – leading to Magna Carta.
- Impact of the Norman Conquest on the village – castle building, feudal system, changes to the lives of the villagers.
- Youngest son of the lord goes off to fight in the Crusades.
- Everyday life in the village – work, law and order, the feudal system on practice, the church and religious beliefs. Simulation of a manor court in action.
- Some of the villagers go on a pilgrimage – transport, religious beliefs, Chaucer.
- Villager commits a crime and runs away to live in a town. Examination of town life: comparison with village life.
- One of villagers is impressed (or joins local stonemason) to help build Edward I's castles in Wales. Follow his story but also look at Wales and developments in castle building.
- Village economy and economic relationship with nearby market town. Buying and selling in the town.

Segments around THE VILLAGE: Peasants' Revolt, Saxon Village, 1066 Events, Impact of Norman Conquest, Everyday life in the village, Town life, Economic relations with town, Castle development, Pilgrimages, Crusades, Magna Carta, Black Death.

Key points to bear in mind when planning units

The programmes of study are merely blocks of content which have no real shape or coherence. This provides teachers with the opportunity to make them their own.

1 **Plan the unit as a whole. Give it an overall shape. Ask unifying questions so that patterns emerge.**

   To give the unit shape and coherence, it is important to develop a focus for it. The focus statement at the beginning of the programme of study can be used or teachers can devise their own.

   One approach is to provide pupils with a range of pictorial sources of different aspects of society – social classes, housing, clothing, work, town and country, and so on – at the beginning of the unit and ask them to discuss what these tell them about the society at the time, for example Britain in 1066 or 1500. Then tell the pupils that at the end of the unit they will be reconsidering their ideas and judgements in the light of all they have studied. Work at the end of the unit could include questions like: how accurate were the early judgements? how much has changed in the period covered by the unit? what has changed most? what periods within the time span saw the most change?

2 **Do not attempt to cover all the content in the same depth: be selective.**

   It has become clear that if teachers attempt to cover all the content in the same depth, this will mean one lesson per topic. Yet much of the most useful and interesting work in history lessons is done when pupils study a unit in some depth and get to know the individuals as real people. This means that it is necessary to carve out some in-depth studies from the programme of study and treat the rest of the unit with broad brush stokes. This will involve reorganising the content of the study unit.

3 **Organise the unit around key questions, problems to be solved and issues to be resolved. Encourage pupils to question stereotypes and accepted views.**

   This is crucial if pupils are to make progress with the concepts and skills in the attainment targets and if coverage of the targets is to be accomplished in an integrated way rather than being tacked on the end. It also provides an opportunity to question the stereotypes handed down by generations of textbooks, for example the three-field system, roles of women and so on. The key questions can be about events which are not named in the programme of study but which allow important parts to be covered. For example, the Gunpowder Plot is not mentioned in the Making of the UK unit but the question 'Were the Catholics framed?' provides the opportunity to cover AT3 skills and important questions about religious differences. The plague in the seventeenth century could be used to look at medical ideas and practices to introduce aspects of the scientific revolution which is part of the programme of study.

4 **Use case studies of individuals, events and places to illustrate and explain concepts.**

   Often in history teaching there are too many generalisations and discussion of 'types' of people. Pupils are more interested in real individuals whom they can get to know. Comparing two monarchs, such as William I and Richard III, will be more engaging than looking at the general development of the medieval monarchy and can be used to raise issues about the changes in the role and position of the monarch.

5 **Brainstorm possible enquiries. Look for real historical issues and topics which will motivate pupils.**

These will identify the areas to be covered in depth. At this stage it is useful to identify an AT focus for each enquiry; will a particular enquiry create opportunities for looking at change, cause, attitudes of the time, different interpretations of the past or the use of sources? It is quite likely that several of these areas will be covered but it is helpful to have a main focus which identifies the principal thrust of the enquiry, for example 'Was King Charles a martyr?' (AT2), 'Were the Catholics framed?' (AT3).

6 **Reduce enquiries to a reasonable number. Check attainment targets.**

It is likely that you will end up with more enquiries than can be taught in one term. It will be necessary to reduce the number to a manageable level. While this is being done, it is important to check that all the attainment targets and the programme of study will be covered. It is helpful at this stage to plot the enquiries on a matrix to check that there will be opportunities to use a range of sources, to pick up cross-curricular themes, gender and multi-cultural issues, and offer the pupils a variety of experiences in and out of the classroom.

7 **Plan work with assessment in mind.**

It is helpful for a department to plan some work common to all teachers. This can be done by agreeing the tasks which will be used for recording purposes. These should include a variety of approaches – work targeted on a single level, work targeted at a range of levels and work ranging across the attainment targets (see Chapter 8). Within this structure and the general aims of each enquiry individual teachers can be allowed flexibility to proceed as they wish.

Activity

Decide what system, matrix or otherwise, that the department is going to use to plan units and ensure that the various elements identified in the National Curriculum are covered.

Identify the next unit which the department is going to teach. Brainstorm the unit and decide upon the main issues or key questions you want to develop as your principal enquiries. Choose one and consider the content involved and how you might teach it. Think about the attainment target(s) this issue might access and how you might adjust your teaching so that the tasks/activities you set access different statements of attainment.

You can then proceed to plan the whole unit. It is worth pointing out that this is a planning exercise and that there are likely to be gaps or vague areas in your matrix which will need attention as you get closer to the actual teaching of the unit.

7 Planning lessons

Having planned a unit and identified enquiries and broad activities, the next stage is to draw up more specific lesson plans. These will have to be more closely related to the attainment targets and assessment of pupils' performance. This could lead to lessons in which a series of highly targeted questions focus on one or several statements of attainment. Whilst there is a place for such work, it would be a great pity if the majority of lessons took on this kind of approach to meet the perceived requirements of the Order. History could become sterile and monotonous.

The Order itself and the *Non-statutory Guidance* in references to teaching methods and enquiry and communication suggest the use of a wide range of approaches. Clearly the authors are anxious not to put teachers in an attainment target/assessment straitjacket and wish to retain flexibility and creativity in the presentation of lessons and the involvement of pupils.

This chapter suggests some ways in which teachers might approach lesson planning to introduce elements of the National Curriculum in a varied and stimulating way. This is obviously highly selective and far from comprehensive; the suggestions are merely starting points. Teachers should consider them alongside the suggestions for activities in the wide variety of textbooks already on the market and the examination of different teaching methods contained in *Implementing the National Curriculum History* (NCC Inset Resources, 1991b).

Scheme of work: The Black Death and the Peasants' Revolt

This section is designed to show how the attainment targets might be accessed in a run of lessons on two topic areas in the Medieval Realms study unit. Some teachers would consider this too detailed, given the time constraints of covering the content in this unit. However, it could be an area treated in more depth because it is an engaging one for pupils and provides good opportunities to cover a range of attainment targets and a variety of levels within them; and it could be used for assessment. Of course, it is not necessary to use all the ideas suggested below; one or two could be incorporated in a scheme of work which occupies less lesson time.

Lesson 1

What was the Black Death and how did it reach Britian?

- Use map to trace movement of Black Death across Europe. Pictorial and written sources describing the disease.
- AT3 levels 1, 2 and 3

Lesson 2

What caused the Black Death?

- Compare medieval views and modern views on causes of the disease. Look at actions medieval people took to avoid catching plague and stop it spreading.
- AT1 strand (c), levels 6 and 7; AT3 levels 1–4

Lesson 3

What were the consequences of the Black Death?

- Examine short- and long-term causes using graphs and statistical data. Focus on effect on medieval villages and position of peasant (economic consequences). Could link up with English department for creative writing or drama department for playlets on the Black Death.
- AT1 strand (b), levels 4, 5 and 6

Lesson 4

What caused the Peasants' Revolt?

- (The following assumes work on life and position of peasant.) Consider long-term causes – labour services, feudal obligations, etc. – together with effects of Black Death and the Statute of Labourers 1351 (how consequences of one event can become causes of another). Then short-term causes – Poll Tax 1381. Pupils write a letter to king setting out their grievances (see example on p. 39).
- AT1 strand (b) levels 2, 3 and 4

Lessons 5 and 6

What happened?

- Use narrative text and sources to trace events. Decision-making exercise – what should the king do? Present pupils with various options for the king such as run away, give in to demands, etc. and the possible consequences. Pupils decide. Conflicting written and pictorial evidence on murders of Chancellor and Archbishop of Canterbury in Tower of London.
- AT3 levels 1–7

Lesson 7

How did the revolt end and what were the consequences?

- Use variety of sources to consider events at Smithfield. Pupils write a biased newspaper account on king's side or peasants' side.
- AT3 levels 3, 4 and 5; AT2 levels 4 and 6
- Consider short- and long-term consequences.
- AT1 strand (b), levels 4 and 5

A few ideas for more engaging lessons

The following are suggestions for different kinds of activities which will involve pupils in active learning and stimulating lessons, whilst also accessing the attainment targets. These activities could be used in many different contexts.

Idea 1

Divide class into groups and give the groups different sets of sources on a particular topic or enquiry. Ask them to report their conclusions back to whole class and discuss how the selection of sources can lead to different interpretations of history (AT2). This activity will also cover a wide range of levels in AT3: communicating information, making deductions from sources, usefulness for particular enquiry, etc.

Example: were the Romans civilised?

Discuss the meaning of the word 'civilised'. To some groups give sources about building, medicine, public health, etc., in Roman times. To others give sources on slavery, gladiators, animals used in arena, etc. Ask the groups to use the sources to decide if the Romans were civilised and to prepare a case to support their views. Debate issue in class. This example also covers AT1 strand (c) (features of past societies).

Idea 2

Write a guide to a castle or a house using historical sources and secondary accounts (AT3 and AT1 strand (c)).

Example: castle guide

Draw up a guide for or take a party of American tourists around a castle and describe the different features of the castle, how the different parts of the castle were used and what castle life was like.

Variations

- Write an estate agent's blurb for a large house, including furniture, stressing all the points which might make it attractive to a potential buyer.
- You are the information officer for a Roman site/medieval castle/seventeeth-century country house. Draw up a pamphlet for schoolchildren visiting the site.

Idea 3

Plan a 'This is Your Life' programme for a particular individual in history, for example Elizabeth I or Winston Churchill. This could be a programme which does a hatchet job on the individual, takes a neutral stance, or is extremely favourable to the person.

Example: Napoleon

Pupils use a variety of sources and textbook accounts to prepare a programme which attacks Napoleon as a power-hungry dictator, or one which shows him as the saviour of France after the chaos of the Revolution and one who introduced many beneficial reforms.

Variation

Pupils write an obituary for a friend or an enemy.

Idea 4

Divide class into two halves and ask one half to develop arguments for and one half arguments against a proposition. Then a debate is held. Pupils have to seek out arguments for their case from textbooks and other sources.

Example: which side should we join in the English Civil War?

One half puts arguments for joining king's side, other half for joining the Parliamentarian side (AT1 strand (b) and AT3);
or
Charles I was a terrible king (AT2).

Idea 5

Ask pupils to put themselves in position of people in different groups in a particular historical period (rich, poor, peasants, merchants, women) and choose a number of objects to put in a time capsule to show people in later times how they lived (AT1 strand (c), AT2, AT3). They should explain the reasons for their choices.

Example: life in the Middle Ages

Pupils identify ten things which a rich person and then a poor person might choose to indicate what his or her life was like in the Middle Ages.

Idea 6

Prepare a documentary programme for radio or television on a particular period or historical event. Pupils have to select written and pictorial evidence to use in the programme and explain their choice of material; they also have to consider the interpretation they have put on programme (AT2, AT1 strand (c), AT3).

Example: the Blitz in the Second World War

Pupils may even use real interviews here and possibly real artefacts from the time.

Idea 7

Pupils create a wall poster about a particular issue or event expressing peoples' views from a particular period (AT1 strand (c), or one which tries to persuade people to a particular course of action.

Example: posters

- Poster using knowledge of peoples' beliefs in the seventeeth century to tell people what is causing the plague and how to avoid it (AT1 strand (c).
- Poster telling people why they should join the revolutionaries against the British in the War of Independence (AT1 strand (b)).

Idea 8

Write one of the following:

- letter
- newspaper account
- letter to a newspaper
- health inspector's report
- diary extract
- speech
- job reference for a political post

There are many variations of this which can be used in different contexts.

Example: letters

A group of peasants have found an old priest who can write. Write a letter to King Richard II setting out the reasons why you (peasants) are unhappy about the Poll Tax and the way things are being run at the moment. Set out your grievances and ask the king for help (AT1 strand (b)).

Write a newspaper account of the Battle of Hastings from a Norman or a Saxon point of view (AT2).

Write a letter to a newspaper protesting about the conditions in factories at the beginning of the nineteenth century. Write a reply from a factory owner (AT1 strand (c)).

8 Assessment

Assessment is probably the area of the National Curriculum which worries teachers most. They are concerned about the form which the SATs will take and how they will be applied. They are concerned about the problem of developing effective teacher assessment which does not involve complex operations, regular examination-style tests and an enormous amount of time. The aim of this section is to help teachers begin the process of developing an approach to assessment which meets the requirements of the National Curriculum and is reasonable in terms of its daily operation.

Work at KS3 will be assessed in two ways.

> 1 At the end of the key stage, probably at the beginning of the summer term, pupils will sit SATs. These will be set externally and marked by teachers using mark schemes which will be provided. The marking will be moderated. The tests will be on core units only.
>
> 2 Throughout the key stage, pupils' work will be assessed by their own teachers. This is, in effect, a form of continuous assessment.

Teacher assessment

There is much confusion about the nature of teacher-based assessment. It should be remembered that it has two roles: to recognise and record pupils' achievements and progress, and to help the teacher to support pupils' learning throughout the key stage. There is nothing new in these requirements. History teachers have always assessed their pupils as a normal part of their teaching. Judgements about what pupils can do, what they are finding difficult and where they should go next have always been part of good practice and an essential part of planning future work. This remains the case under the National Curriculum. What is different is that whereas this was usually done informally, it must now be done formally within the context of the programmes of study and the attainment targets.

The following points should be borne in mind.

> 1 Teacher assessment should not be an activity which is separate from normal classroom work.
>
> 2 When planning a unit and tasks, the programme of study and the attainment targets should be regarded as interdependent.
>
> 3 All three attainment targets should be accessed in a unit several times but not necessarily in any particular activity. The tasks in an activity may focus on one attainment target, although, quite naturally, there will usually be opportunities to bring in other attainment targets.

> 4 The starting point for any task should be the issues and questions which arise naturally from the content – the questions which you, or the pupils, think are interesting ones to ask about the content. If you set up issues for the pupils to investigate, problems for them to solve, or historical controversies for them to consider, then the attainment targets will follow and the pupils will be more motivated.
>
> 5 The levels of attainment are not designed as hurdles which have to be cleared just once. Nor is it the case that pupils master one level before they can move on to the next. Pupils will return to levels again and again in a variety of contexts and using materials of varying degrees of complexity. There is no magic formula which sets out how many times each level must be attained before pupils can be judged to have achieved that level. This is a matter for the professional judgement of the teacher.
>
> 6 To help the teacher make this judgement, attainment should be recorded throughout the key stage thus building up a profile of the pupils' attainment and progress.

Teacher assessment should not require the use of special assessment tasks or examination-style tests. Much, if not all, of the normal work planned for pupils should relate to the skills and understandings in the attainment targets. Therefore, much of the normal work completed by pupils will not only foster their skills and understandings but also provide the teacher with evidence of what each pupil can do in relation to the attainment targets.

Some teachers have found themselves in the position where they have to devise special assessment tasks or tests because their normal work does not cover the full range of the attainment targets and their constituent levels. This usually happens because of a lack of careful planning. If a unit is organised around a number of key questions, there will be plenty of opportunites to access the attainment targets. Additional tasks can be added if this is not the case.

Example

A scheme of work for three lessons on the Battle of Hastings could be organised around the following key questions.

> - If you were Harold of Wessex in 1066, would you guard the south coast against William or the north-east coast against Harold Hardrada, or split your forces and guard both? (AT1 strand (b)
> - Look at the relative positions of William and Harold after the Battle of Stamford Bridge. Harold has just fought one hard battle and now has to march his army hundreds of miles south where William is waiting with his army. Who is favourite to win? (AT1 strand (b)
> - Were there any moments during the battle when Harold could have won? (AT1 strand (b)

> - How did Harold die? (AT3)
> - Why did William win? Was it because of his own skill, because Harold made mistakes, or because he was unlucky? Or was it a combination of all three? (AT1 strand (b)

In this example, the attainment targets are accessed while genuine and worthwhile historical questions have been posed. No attempt has been made to cover all the attainment targets. There is an emphasis on AT1 strand (b) (cause and consequence). This does not matter as long as planning ensures that the other attainment targets are covered elsewhere in the unit. As most history teachers will be aware, there is no problem in finding work for AT2 and AT3 on the Battle of Hastings.

Assessment through a variety of tasks

There should be as much variety as possible in the types of tasks set for pupils as the basis for assessment. These can be expressed in terms of the attainment targets and the statements of attainment.

- Tasks set on one statement of attainment.
- A series of tasks which take pupils through consecutive statements in one attainment target.
- A series of tasks which focus on one attainment target but does not access the levels in consecutive order. Each task may access a range of levels. By the end of the exercise many levels will have been accessed.
- More open-ended tasks which access a range of levels, where the work is targeted on the attainment target in general rather than on particular levels.
- Open-ended activities which range across a number of attainment targets.

Examples

1 Tasks set on one statement of attainment

This can be a helpful approach when one wants to introduce a new idea or skill to pupils. It can also be useful when trying to keep close control of the assessment of pupils' progress. Teachers will find innumerable opportunites for this in their schemes of work, for example, how did castles change from the eleventh to the fourteenth centuries? (AT1a, level 3)

It is also an appropriate approach for statements of attainment which appear to have little relationship with levels above and below them and could be missed out altogether unless targeted specifically, for example distinguishing between a fact and an opinion (AT4, level 3). One way of assessing this level could be as follows.

Provide pupils with four statements:

i. William was Duke of Denmark.
ii. William had the best claim to the throne of England.
iii. William invaded England in September 1066.
iv. William was the best medieval king.

Pupils could check which of these statements are correct (for research or homework). They will probably agree about statements (i) and (iii) but disagree about statements (ii) and (iv) with some pupils deciding they could not check these at all. Class discussion about the reasons for this should lead some pupils to realise that the agreement/disagreement is due to the different nature of the statements.

2 **A series of tasks which takes pupils through consecutive statements in one attainment target.**

Consider Sources F, G and H on p. 44 for assessment of levels in AT3.

AT3 Level		Task set
1	Communicate information from a source.	What can you see in the picture? (source F) Draw up an inventory for the bedroom shown in source F.
2	Sources can stimulate and help answer questions about the past.	In what ways does source F help us find out how people lived? How can we find out how people lived? What questions would you like to ask about source F?
3	Make deductions from sources.	Are the people in the picture (source F) rich or poor? How do you know?
4	Put together information from different historical sources.	Compare the rooms shown in sources F and G and the inventory in source H. What do they suggest about the difference between rich and poor families?
5	Usefulness of a source (content).	Does source F (or G or H) tell you about how clean and hygienic, how rich, how religious people were, how large families were in the sixteenth century?
6	Compare usefulness.	Which tells you more about life at home – source G or source H? Choose five things that best show what life was like for (i) a poor person and (ii) a rich person. Explain your choices. (This task assumes work on life in the sixteenth century.)

ASSESSMENT

Source F

A bedroom in the sixteenth century

Source G

A kitchen in the sixteenth century

Source H

> 1 boarded bedstead, 1 mattress, 1 bolster, 1 pillow, 1 pair of sheets, 1 bed blanket.
> 2 salt boxes, 1 frying pan, 1 pair of tongs and a roasting iron, 1 kettle, 1 saw, 3 spoons, 2 wooden plates, 5 dishes and 2 earthen pots, 1 stone pot.
> A little table, 2 stools, 3 chisels and 2 hammers, 2 pairs of hand cuffs and 1 dozen handkerchiefs, 2 old shirts.

The inventory of Thomas Herries, who died in 1599

3 **A series of tasks which focus on one attainment target. Each task accesses a range of levels but not necessarily in consecutive order.**

This will apply to a wide range of tasks as key questions quite naturally bring in different levels of questions. However, it is often the case that different questions will pick up different combinations of levels, for example AT3 levels 3, 4 and 7, or AT2 levels 4 and 6.

> This series of questions were based on three sources about the murder of Thomas Becket: an account of the murder by Edward Grim, a priest who was present; an account by William Fitzstephen, Becket's clerk; and a painting of the murder made in the following century.
>
> - How do the written accounts of the murder differ? (AT3 levels 1, 3 and 4)
> - What evidence is there that both writers were on Becket's side? (AT3 level 3)
> - Does this mean that their accounts cannot be trusted? (AT3 levels 7 and 8)
> - Is there any evidence that Becket wanted to die? (AT3 level 3)
> - Do you think the painting is a reliable source? (AT3 level 7)
> - What gives you the best idea of what happened: the written accounts or the painting? (AT3 levels 2, 5 and 6)
> - Who do you think was to blame for Becket's death: Henry, Becket, or the knights who killed him? Explain your answer. (AT3 levels 3, 7 and 10)

4 **More open-ended tasks which access a range of levels in an attainment target but not necessarily in consecutive order.**

Here it is more important to target work on the attainment target in general rather than on particular levels. Assessment would be based very much on the outcome of work which could be quite different between pupils. A good example of this is the work on William and the Battle of Hastings which can be seen at the beginning of this chapter. The different key questions could lead to answers which hit a variety of levels. To some extent this will depend on the way this run of lessons is introduced and the other materials provided.

5 **Open-ended tasks which range across a number of attainment targets.**

These will often be the most exciting and motivating exercises in the classroom and can provide evidence of a wide range of skills and understanding. However, it can sometimes be difficult to draw comparisons across the class for record-keeping purposes.

> - Plan a 'This is Your Life' programme for Bonnie Prince Charlie. This could be very critical of him or favourable to him or try to be neutral. Include items like: should he have rebelled? did he have a claim to the throne? did he make mistakes? what does he have to say for himself? Write a script and include details about who you will invite, what they will be asked and what they will say. (AT3 and AT2)
> - Peasants' Revolt 1381 – a group of peasants have found an old priest who can write. Write a letter to King Richard II telling him about the problems you face and why the Poll Tax is unfair. Set out in your letter your grievances about the way things are run in 1381 and what changes you would like to see. Ask the king for his help. (AT1 strands (a), (b) and (c); AT3)

It is important that these more open-ended tasks are used. There is a danger that pupils could be faced with a diet of tasks which are targeted on just one level and which look like examination questions. In these sorts of questions there is generally little scope for anything more than a five- or six-line answer. Such a diet would be extremely boring for pupils and teachers. Although it is necessary to set up tasks which can be assessed, we should not allow a narrow concept of assessment to determine the whole pattern of our teaching. The answer to this is to use a variety of different approaches and to make sure that within these there is sufficient opportunity to assess pupils' work in relation to the full range of the attainment targets.

The enquiry and communication aspect of the history Order requires teachers to be concerned about the way pupils communicate historical knowledge and understanding. It suggests different forms that these could take – planning and writing extended narratives, descriptions and explanations, summarising results of historical investigations, taking part in debates and so on. These, and other activities like role plays, wall displays, etc., can only be achieved through activities which are more openly constructed and likely to access a range of levels of attainment. This has implications for assessment.

- Much of this work will have a written product which sometimes may be difficult to assess comparatively across a whole class. In this case it will be up to the professional judgement of the teacher (as it has always been) to decide how to apply and credit levels of attainment in different attainment targets. Such work could be produced individually, in pairs or in groups. If the work is produced in conjunction with other pupils, it is important to be able to identify the contributions of individual pupils. In some cases, such as a wall display or group magazine, this may be relatively easy but in other cases it may involve watching a group work to identify individual contributions.

- Monitoring or observing pupils in action has always been part of a teacher's repertoire for making judgements about a pupil's performance. This could involve making rough notes during or after a lesson about any noticeable attainment during a class discussion or similar activity, or deciding before the lesson to target particular pupils to observe for recording purposes. This is particularly important for those pupils who never do well in their written work.

> ### Activity
>
> **Looking at pupils' work**
>
> The extracts of pupils' work in Figure 7 were written in response to an exercise on the problems facing the Roman Empire at the end of the fourth century. The Y7 pupils were presented with a range of sources, primary and secondary, and a map showing the Empire and the barbarian tribes which were threatening it. The pupils were asked to identify the problems from the sources and to try to think of possible solutions. They were then asked to set this out in the form of a discussion paper to be presented to the emperor.
>
> Read the extracts and discuss the following.
>
> - Which attainment targets are covered in the answers?
> - Which levels would you award the pupils?
> - How might you record this?

Discussion

You will probably identify AT1 strand (b) and AT3. The use of sources clearly brings in AT3 but the skills in this area are being used very much as servicing skills. The exercise as such does not focus on AT3. The first decision to make, therefore, is whether to record against AT3. There will be many other opportunities to cover AT3.

If we agree that the main focus of the exercise is AT1 (b), then we must ask: how well does this exercise access this strand of AT1? To do the task pupils have to say what was causing problems for the Empire (ultimately contributing to its downfall) and explain how these were causing the problems. The pupils also have to suggest possible solutions and show how these solutions are related to the problems.

So, which levels are being accessed here? There do appear to be opportunities for pupils to show multi-causal understanding (level 4) and how causes are related (level 7). Moreover, we might say that relating solutions to problems is an aspect of the same level. It involves the same sort of thought process and would form part of a general consideration of why things happen – how not adopting certain solutions can help bring about an event. It is important not to stick too rigidly to the exact wording of the statements of attainment: this will lead to a very narrow experience for the pupils. It is perfectly reasonable to look for equivalents of a level and this appears to be one.

Some pupils might even begin to put the problems into some kind of order of importance (level 6), but the question does not directly invite this and you cannot conclude from pupils' failure to do this that they cannot do it. The same is true with identifying different types of causes (level 5). You could follow up this exercise with more direct questions designed to focus pupils' attention on these two areas.

Figure 7: *Extracts of pupils' work*

Problems of the Empire

Honorius I know you have many problems in the Empire. I have given solutions to these problems in this. The Worst problem you have in the is the vast amount of money you spend on the army. The solution to this problem is to simply lower the taxes. There fore the soldiers do not need so much to feed their families. This would also control the extremly high taxes. Another major problem is those uncivilised barbarians. The Solution to this problem is to let so many in. From places like Germany. Their should be roughly about 5 hundred barbarians in one year. Once a barbarian has crossed the border he or she will learn the ways of the Romans. Another Concerning matter is the growth of the Empire. The Empire has reached its maxium height and can not grow any more. This is a very difficult situation. Though I have thought long and hard and have come up with a good solution. The Solution includes with drawing Asia minor because this piece of land does not give the Empire very much. It does not give jewels or supplies so it would not hurt the Empire if you withdrawed from this land. Another problem I have noticed about the Empire is the old defensive system. The old defensive system has a major problem. It does not work any more. It is beginning to become a large threat to the Empire if it isn't solved. The only thing that you can do is to make a new defensive system. I have an Idea. Cover all your borders with stone walls. Then set traps inwould in the stone walls. This is probably sure to work. Then if any remainders of soldiers are left fire arrows with your brilliant bows men. Another problem which you face is the crime in the Empire. More and more people are stealing. Well a lowering of prices of goods should keep the crime at a reasonable rate.

                Yours sincerly Problem Solver

Letter to the Emperor

Dear Emperor

I am sorry to say that I have noticed many problems in your empire such as

- Tax rises
- Cost of the Army
- Limit of expansion
- Supply problems
- Barbarian Attacks
- Poor defence systems
- Greed
- Civil wars
- Crimes

you could stop these problems by:

- Paying army loss
- Bringing down taxes
- More efficient supply systems
- Attack the barbarians if they attack you
- Get better defence systems
- Kill greedy people
- Introduce peace
- having harsher punishments for criminals

Problems in the empire

O, greatest emperor, your humble servant begs you to change somethings around here. Me and my fellow colleagues implore you to

- Give free land and weapons to settlers on the borders.
- Press gang people into the army to stop the problem of not enough men.
- Charge more tax on the rich to stop rich people from spending to much.
- Let the poor have certain limits of time to pay their taxes so then it would not be so high.
- Build strong walls and forts on the frontiers to toughen it.
- Denounce the governors and appoint more unselfish ones.
- You, emperor, should not spend so much money on the army and spend it on other things
- And finally you should get rid of disonest laws. here, o emperor, I end my letter and hope yous will take heed of my suggestions.

When considering the pupils' responses, a number of questions are raised.

- Is a longer answer a better answer?
- Does an answer which provides more detailed explanation of each point merit a higher level?
- Does a fuller explanation of one area of problems and solutions (as in one extract) rate higher than a list of several problems and solutions where the connections have not been drawn in another extract?
- Can you record a level where the understanding appears to be implied in the answer but is not explicitly stated?
- What can you expect of Y7 pupils at these levels?
- How do you record the levels? (See section on Recording on p. 51.)

Marking

While it is clear that a teacher should be building up a profile of pupils' achievements in a mark book or a record card, the question remains about what to put on pupils' work. The old practice of a number or letter grade has obvious shortcomings, the main one being that it does not tell pupils much about what they have achieved and what they should aim to achieve in the future.

Some teachers argue that it is not necessary to place any kind of grade on work as long as there is a constructive comment which points the way forward for the pupil. However, others will not agree with this or be constrained by whole-school policy. If grades are used, it is important that the department decides whether they are for attainment or effort, or whether a separate grade should be given for these.

The attainment grade should be related to specific targets and not just an impressionistic mark. It is also important that pupils receive regular comments on their work. The usefulness of telling pupils that they have reached AT3 level 1 must be doubted; it could lead to confusion, expecially if they are awarded different levels – higher and lower – at different times. It would be more useful to write something like: 'You have described what these people are wearing carefully and accurately but you should also try to work out from what they are wearing whether they are rich or poor.' (AT3 level 1–3) This tells them what they have achieved and where to go next. It might only be possible to write such comments for each pupil every two or three weeks.

Involving pupils in their assessment

It is suggested by the School Examination and Assessment Council (SEAC) that pupils are involved in their own assessment and that opportunities are provided for teachers to review pupils' work and progress with them at regular intervals. This would provide for many a more effective form of assessment than simple comments on work. Of course, many teachers already do this in a more informal way when handing back work or marking work with pupils.

In the context of the National Curriculum, this would mean that pupils would need to know more about statements of attainment and how their work relates to these. No-one would wish on pupils any kind of detailed exposition of the National Curriculum, but they could be informed over a longish period of time about the different levels of attainment and how they should be trying to achieve these, for example looking at several causes and how these are interrelated. This would also mean that pupils should be given some explanation of the purposes of tasks when they are set so that they can have a grasp of the learning objectives of an exercise as well as the immediate content of the exercise, for example the causes of the Peasants' Revolt.

Recording

History, as a National Curriculum subject, falls within the general requirements for recording and reporting. This means that all pupils must be given a written report each year. However, there is no statutory requirement to report level scores in these annual reports. Some departments might find it a helpful exercise to make judgements about pupils at the end of each year, especially if classes will be getting new teachers. Whether these judgements are made available to parents will depend on the general school policy. If they are, then it is important that parents are made aware of the fact that these are based on teacher assessment and are not part of the SATs which take place at the end of the key stage.

It is only at the end of KS3 that the pupils are reported against the levels: the first cohort reaching this point in the spring/summer of 1994. It is the case, however, that parents can ask at any time for information about their child's progress in each attainment target. This information must be provided within fifteen days.

Subject specific requirements for history have not yet been finalised. Matters such as rules of aggregation within AT1 (whether/how the levels in three strands are combined to give one level for AT1) and across all the attainment targets will have to be decided. Many teachers have found it useful in the meantime to record each attainment target separately and each strand of AT1 separately. The question of aggregation can thus be left till later on.

Although it should be possible to use any of the normal work set for evidence of a pupil's progress, it is impractical to try to record attainment for every piece of work. Also some exercises will not work; they will not achieve the expected responses from the pupils or achieve any record-worthy results. Whatever the reasons for this, the rule must be: if it doesn't work, don't use it for recording purposes.

Some selection must be made. It is strongly suggested here that this selection should be made from normal classroom work, although teachers can, if they wish, set special assessment tasks during or at the end of each unit covering all the attainment targets. It is helpful if a department can agree on the tasks to be used for recording purposes as it allows for moderation within the school. The tasks selected should cover a range of attainment targets and levels, and use a variety of different types of activities. Whatever the method chosen, the aim must be to have several recordings against each attainment target by the end of the year. The recordings should be shown in a mark book or on a separate record card. This can be pupil-based or attainment-target based. In the former, each pupil would have a card and against tasks pupils would be given the levels they have been awarded for particular attainment targets. In the latter, the attainment targets and the three separate strands of AT1 would be set out across a double page or A3-sized sheet with the pupils' names down the side of the page (or several pages). Tasks would be listed under the attainment targets and the pupils would be awarded a level, as in Figure 8.

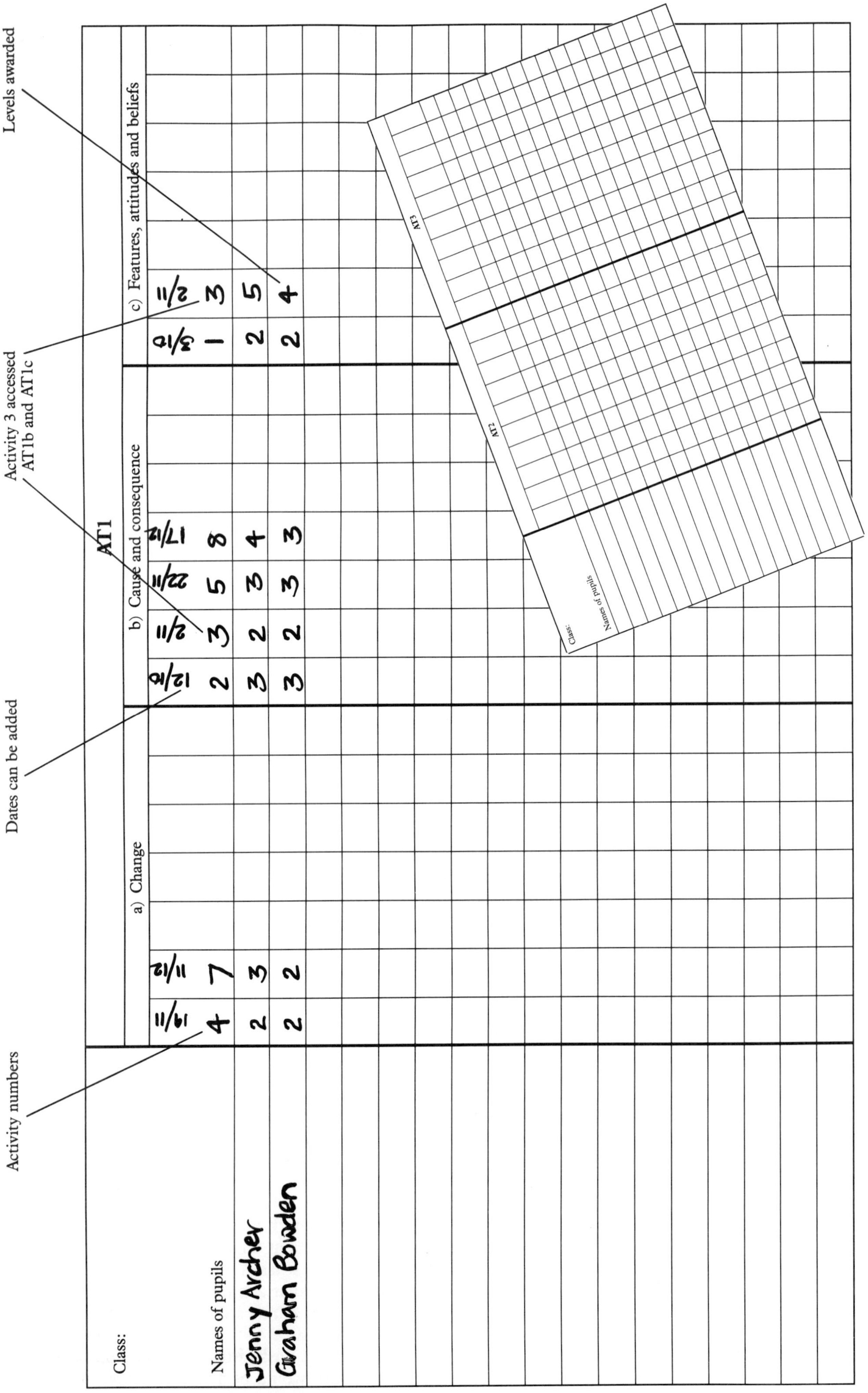

ASSESSMENT

Figure 8: *One possible way of setting out a mark book or record card. It is designed to fit on A3-sized paper*

		a) Change				b) Cause and consequence					c) Features, attitudes and beliefs		
Class:						AT1							
Names of pupils		19/11	11/12			12/16	11/2	11/22	17/12		12/16	2/11	
Jenny Archer		4	7			2	3	5	8		1	3	
Graham Bowden		2	3			3	2	3	4		2	5	
		2	2			3	2	3	3		2	4	

Labels:
- Activity numbers
- Dates can be added
- Activity 3 accessed AT1b and AT1c
- Levels awarded

(Overlaid card shows: Class, Names of Pupils, AT1, AT2, AT3)

In both these methods of recording, there would need to be some description of the activities themselves including details of the tasks, how much support was provided, top and bottom levels accessed and so on. One simple way to do this is to number activities or tasks selected for recording purposes, date them, and put them in a file with comments as soon as they are completed. The numbers of the activities are then put on the record sheet under the relevant attainment target or strand of AT1 (as shown in Figure 8). If an activity covers more than one attainment target, it is recorded under both.

Whenever teachers wish to see what the assessment tasks were and the range and type of materials used, etc., they can look in the file. In some cases this may simply mean putting in a reference to pages and tasks used in a textbook. This is very useful for reference at the end of the year when making a summative judgement about the pupils' perfomance and is very helpful in cataloguing progression, for example showing how pupils perform as support is removed.

Making judgements

Drawing up marking schemes to assess and record performance within and across levels is a difficult area. There is no point in devising an approach which is too time-consuming to carry out. Matters are also complicated by the nature of the attainment targets. For some attainment targets, it might be possible to use a series of levels as a marking scheme, for example in AT1 strand (b), where some pupils might respond with a single causal explanation, others with a multi-causal explanation, and others might categorise causes or argue that some are more important than others. But, in general, the different levels do not provide and were not intended to be marking schemes. This means that for many tasks it is more appropriate to target one or two levels and draw up a marking scheme appropriate to those levels. Such a scheme might identify different levels at which the statement of attainment (level 3, 4 etc.) can be achieved.

For example, if we consider AT3 level 3 – making deductions from historical sources – we might ask the following questions about what constitutes attainment at this level.

- Does the deduction have to be valid?
- Are some deductions better than others – less obvious, more important, more to the point, etc.
- Should there be one or more than one deduction?
- Is the deduction made from writing or a pictorial source or from both?
- Does the deduction have to refer back to the source?
- How many sources?
- How difficult or demanding are the sources?
- How direct was the question asked?

This might lead to a marking scheme as follows:

- No level – Invalid deduction
- L1 – Single unsupported valid deduction
- L2 – Several unsupported valid deductions
- L3 – Single supported deduction
- L4 – Several supported deductions

It is important for the department to reach agreement on what constitutes attainment at a particular level given the range and complexity of sources, types of questions used, etc. and award levels accordingly.

It will happen that some pupils show attainment at higher levels before they have shown attainment at lower levels. This should be welcomed but it should usually be taken as evidence that the pupil is beginning to make progress with the idea or skill rather than as evidence of attainment at that level. It is by no means rare to find eleven-year-olds showing that they can evaluate sources (AT3 level 7), but if they are doing this before they have shown much evidence of attainment at lower levels, then it may be that the exercise is not pitched at an appropriate level of difficulty. It would, however, be a peculiar way to teach history if one did not allow Y7 pupils to do some evaluation of sources (AT3 level 7). To show that this was level 7 against an easy piece of work, it could be recorded as 7? It should be recorded in some form as it allows teachers to track a pupil's progress. This is why it is useful to keep a note of each activity and the context in which tasks were set.

Summative judgement

At the end of the year, it is likely that each pupil will have shown attainment across a number of levels, for example from 2 to 8. How can an overall judgement be made?

1 Whatever judgement you make will only be provisional. Don't feel that you are making a definitive statement about the attainment of the pupil.

2 No judgements at the end of the year or at the end of a key stage will be exact. It is simply not possible to say that Jenny Smith is definitely level 7, and definitely not level 6 or level 8. For some of the time, her performance would have been at level 6 or 8 or 5 depending on all sorts of factors, not least the nature of the tasks set. What you are doing is making a judgement about which level best represents her general attainment.

3 There is no mechanical formula which can be used to reach a summative judgement from the profile on a card. It is not the case of saying that a pupil must have reached level 4 five times before you can judge that he or she has attained level 4. It is rather a matter of professional judgement. The requirement might be more to do with the contexts in which pupils have shown attainment – different content, different kinds of tasks, different activities and so on. But the most important element is the teacher's knowledge of the pupil.

When making a summative judgment at the end of the year, you could use:

- the profile on the record card (taking into account the context and nature of the tasks and activites set);
- the pupil's exercise book or folder;
- your professional knowledge of the pupils.

The last two items can be used to interpret the evidence on the record card to arrive at the levels you think best represent the pupil's perfomance.

Recommended reading

> DES (1985) *History in the Primary and Secondary Years: An HMI view.*

Although written before the National Curriculum, this book contains sections on different aspects of history teaching which are pertinent to planning and teaching NC history.

> Dickinson, A. K., Lee, P. J. and Rogers, P. J. (1984) *Learning History.* Heinemann

Includes chapters from various contributors on teaching history and assessment. Material still relevant to National Curriculum although the book was written some time ago.

> Fiehn, T. (1991) *Time and Money.* BP Education Service, PO Box 30, Blacknest, Alton, Hants, GU34 4PX

A resource pack including pupils' book, teachers' guide, slides and a game which helps teachers to deliver the cross-curricular theme of economic and industrial understanding through history. Would form a strong component for the Expansion, Trade and Industry unit in KS3.

> Lomas, T. (1990) *Teaching and Assessing Historical Understanding.* Teaching of History Series No. 63, Historical Association

An Historical Association pamphlet.

> NCC (1991a) *History Non-statutory Guidance.* National Curriculum Council

Complements and provides further clarification on the meaning of the National Curriculum history Order. Also gives advice on planning, cross-curricular links, etc.

> NCC (1991b) *Implementing National Curriculum History*, NCC Inset Resources. National Curriculum Council

This book accompanies four television programmes produced by Yorkshire Television in conjuction with the National Curriculum Council. Both are designed to help teachers implement the National Curriculum for history.

> Portal, C. (ed.) (1987) *The History Curriculum for Teachers*. Falmer Press

Although pre-National Curriculum, it contains useful chapters on areas such as teaching historical skills and concepts which can be related to the attainment targets.

> Portal, C. (ed.) for the Teaching History Research Group (1992) *Sources in History*. Longman

Includes chapters on the issues involved in developing and assessing pupils' abilities to work with historical sources.

> Schools History Project, Trinity and All Saints' College *Discoveries*. SHP, Brownberrie Lane, Horsforth, Leeds

This is a journal for KS3 history. It is published twice a year and contains advice on teaching and assessing National Curriculum history. Contributions reflect classroom experience of implementing the National Curriculum.

> Shephard, C. (ed.) (1992) *Societies in Change* (Teachers' Resource Book). John Murray

Accompanies pupils' book of the same title. Contains strategies for accessing attainment targets and assessing and recording pupils' work. These are all linked to a wide range of activities in the pupils' book.

> Teaching History Research Group (1991) *How to Plan, Teach and Assess History in the National Curriculum.*

This book contains chapters on planning and assessing work at key stages 1, 2 and 3 and a chapter dedicated to local history in the National Curriculum.

> White, C. (1992) *Assessment in History Teaching: A handbook for secondary teachers.* Longman

Focuses on issues associated with assessment at GCSE but has a short section on assessment for NC history.

> White, C. and Medley, R. (1992) *Planning National Curriculum Assessment in History Teaching for Key Stage 3.* Teaching of History Series No. 67, Historical Association

An Historical Association pamphlet.

> Wilson, M. D. (1985) *History for Pupils with Learning Difficulties.* Hodder and Stoughton

Practical advice on teaching and planning lessons for pupils with learning difficulties.